Art & Artists

THROUGH THE CENTURIES

Authors

Michelle M. McAuliffe and Marsha W. Black

Editor
Karen Tam Froloff

Managing Editor
Karen Goldfluss, M.S. Ed.

Editor-in-Chief
Sharon Coan, M.S. Ed.

Illustrators
Sue Fullam
Bruce Hedges
Michelle M. McAuliffe
Marsha W. Black

Cover Artist
Lesley Palmer

Art Coordinator
Denice Adorno

Imaging
Rosa C. See

Product Manager
Phil Garcia

Publishers
Rachelle Cracchiolo, M.S. Ed.
Mary Dupuy Smith, M.S. Ed.

Teacher Created Materials, Inc.
6421 Industry Way
Westminster, CA 92683
www.teachercreated.com.

ISBN-0-7439-3081-9

Reprinted, 2002
Made in U.S.A.

Table of Contents

Introduction

The human mind has a need to express itself. Some students express thought verbally through the use of language. Others express thought visually by exercising their imagination to create something tangible using line and color. *Art & Artists Through the Centuries* addresses the need for students to express themselves visually, as they learn to appreciate artists and their well-known works.

This book is designed to help teachers impart art history and help the students discern individual artist's techniques. This process enhances learning and assists the student in remembering the artist and the method used to create his/her masterpiece.

The goal is to develop art appreciation, cultural awareness, and social growth that will ultimately becomes a permanent part of the student's education.

How to Use This Book

Art & Artists Through the Centuries is designed for those who wish to give young people an appreciation for fine art by analyzing artists' techniques. Teachers are given a specific way to help students recognize artists' styles so that they may readily identify additional works of an artist by recalling that artist's technique.

This is accomplished by pointing out and explaining elements of an artist's paintings that seem to recur in other works by that artist. When the teacher ascertains that the students understand and can recognize the elements in a painting that are unique to that artist, the students are encouraged to imitate the technique in an original work of their own.

The book is versatile and may be simplified for younger children yet detailed enough to consider the needs of older students.

Each lesson consists of a biography of the featured artist, a vocabulary of words that may be unfamiliar to the student, followed by a commentary on the technique of the artist. When the teacher is assured that the concept of technique is clear, the book gives suggestions for one or more projects, followed by a list of materials needed, along with directions for completing the projects.

The teacher is given guidelines for evaluating the project, a series of test questions, and answers to determine the student's comprehension. The authors also give an illustration of an original work using a particular artist's style in every lesson, as a further aid to teacher and students. The aim of the lessons in this book is to give the teacher material to help students recognize and retain the artists' modes of expression.

At the end of this book are blank lesson forms. The teacher can use these to prepare lessons about artists not included in this book.

Time Line

1,000,000–60,000 B.C.

Aboriginal Rock Art

20,000–10,000 B.C.

Altamira Cave Art

1300 A.D.

Icons

1400 A.D.

Fra Angelico (1387–1455)

1500 A.D.

Pieter Bruegel the Elder (ca.1525–1569)
El Greco (Domenikos Theotokopoulos, 1541–1614)
Diego Velasquez (1599–1660)

1700 A.D.

J. M. W. (Joseph Mallord William) Turner (1775–1857)
Gioacchino Barberi (1783–1857)

1800 A.D.

Berthe Morisot (1841–1895)
Vincent Van Gogh (1853–1890)
Georges Seurat (1859–1891)
Grandma Moses (Anna Mary Roberston, 1860–1961)
Georges Rouault (1871–1958)
Paul Klee (1879–1940)
Pablo Picasso (1881–1973)
Georges Braque (1882–1963)
Amedeo Modigliani (1884–1920)
Diego Rivera (1886–1957)
Marcel Duchamp (1887–1968)
Marc Chagall (1887–1985)
Chang Dai–chien (1899–1983)

1900 A.D.

Lee Krasner (Born in 1908)
Romare Bearden (1912–1988)
Elaine Fried de Kooning (1920–1989)
Quang Ho (Born in 1963)

Creating Rock Art is Where to Start

The Aborigines of Australia

The Aborigines of Australia are some of the oldest people known to man. The various tribes may have existed c. 60,000 years B.C. Some historians place the tribes at 100,000 B.C. They have no written language. They pass their culture and history to succeeding generations through songs, stories, and artwork.

The Aborigines used stories to explain their environment and their own existence. What is the purpose of human life? Why are things around us as they are? When, where, and how did things begin? They have a word for this body of stories which is not translatable in English. The nearest words we have to describe this collection of myths is The Aboriginal Dreamtime, which encompasses the past, present, and future.

Vocabulary

- ***The Aboriginal Dreamtime***

  stories of the Aborigine people and the creation of their world in the distant past, the present time, and in the future

- **rock art**

  polychrome pictographs painted on the walls of caves and beneath rock ledges

- **x-ray style**

  Aboriginal sketches of deer, fish, and other animals showing their spine, liver, heart, lungs, and other internal organs

- **bark painting**

  bark that is treated into flattened pieces and painted on

- **polychrome pictographs**

  an ancient or prehistoric drawing or painting of many colors on a rock wall

- **Aborigine**

  an original inhabitant of a place (i.e., Australia) as opposed to invading or colonizing people

Creating Rock Art is Where to Start *(cont.)*

Technique of the Aborigines

Paintings were sometimes a combination of incising and painting. Brushes were made from sticks that were chewed on one end until they were frayed and brush-like. Colors were red, yellow, and brown and white, gray, and black.

Carvings were incised or chipped out in fragments with a stone, or dug out deeply in an intaglio technique.

Suggestions for a Project

Project 1

To create rock art, students will use a smooth pebble to make a hunting or fishing scene, or draw an animal using the incising technique.

Materials Needed

smooth pebbles (washed), pencil, magic markers

Directions

Wash and dry pebbles. Pencil in geometric stick figure or a hunting/fishing scene. Finish scene by applying small dots, using magic markers.

Project 2

On white paper, students will create x-ray art by drawing the internal organs of a fish, animal of choice, or a person.

Materials Needed

white drawing paper, pencil, eraser, black ballpoint pen, narrow black marker, book showing animal's internal organs

Directions

Use a pencil to draw an animal on white drawing paper. Fill in the animal's organs (heart, liver, lungs, spine, etc.). Use a library book for reference. Trace the outline of the animal with a thin black magic marker. Outline the internal organs with a thin black ballpoint pen.

Creating Rock Art is Where to Start *(cont.)*

Suggestions for a Project *(cont.)*

Project 3

Students will do bark painting by drawing a scene from nature such as sun, moon, stars, river, ocean, weather, etc. Then they will write a story telling how that thing came to be.

Materials Needed

cardboard from corrugated box, crayons or colored chalk, pencils, eraser, fixative, bowl of water, paper towels

Directions

On a piece of brown corrugated box, students sketch a scene from nature. When planning the picture, have them consider the colors to be used: red, yellow, brown, white, black, and gray. Students may use either chalk or crayon. If using chalk, they should dampen surface slightly with paper towel before beginning. When dry, spray with fixative.

Evaluation: Interpretation of the Artist's Technique

1. Did the student use the dot technique in the rock art?
2. Did the student draw internal organs and use wide and narrow lines effectively in the x-ray art?
3. Did the student use only colors allowed and draw a scene from nature in the bark art?

Test Questions

1. What does the term *Aborigine* mean?
2. What is *The Aboriginal Dreamtime*?
3. How do the Aborigines record their history?

Answers to Test Questions

1. An Aborigine is an original inhabitant of a place such as Australia.
2. *The Aboriginal Dreamtime* is a body of stories by the Aborigines about their world.
3. The Aborigines have no written language; therefore, what is known about them is from oral history, stories, songs, and their art.

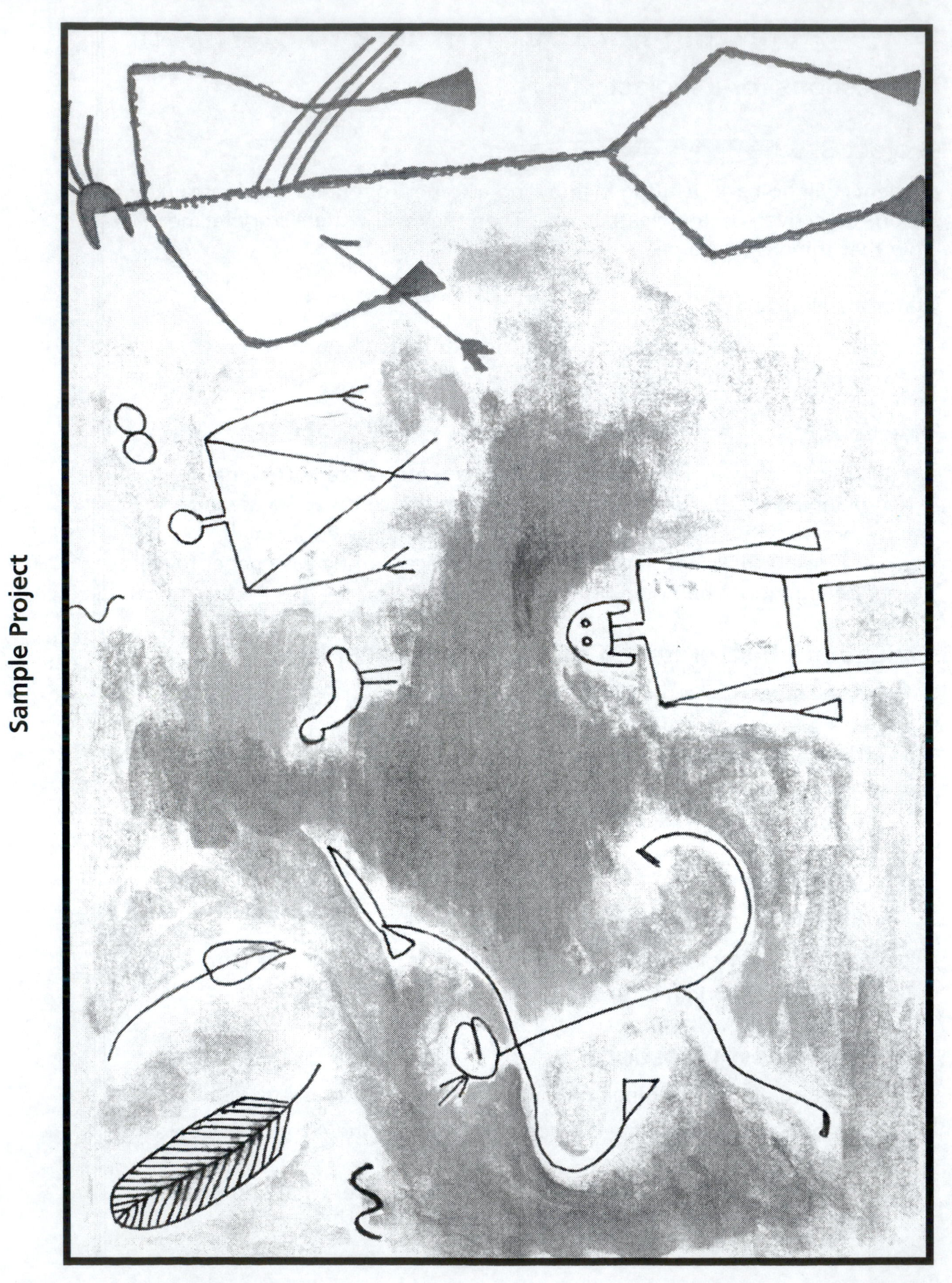

Sample Project

Dispatch a Cache of Cave Art

Cave Art of Altamira

The cave paintings of Altamira are located in Northern Spain in the deep recesses of mountain caves. There they are protected from weathering caused by wind, ice, and precipitation. The paintings are thought to be between 10,000 and 20,000 years old. The paintings are very beautiful and are known as "the Sistine Chapel of Paleolithic Art." The paintings have remained almost the same as when the cave artists put them on the cavern walls.

Cave art is not the only sign of human habitation. These early dwellers, thought to be of the Magdalenian culture, left behind their tools, hearths, and even bits of food. How did these early artists preserve their paintings for posterity? They used natural colors from the earth—ochres and oxides, applied them carefully, and protected them from the elements. They also used crushed animals, plants, and bones in their paints. It is not known why cave artists drew animals inside and overlapping previously drawn animals. The early cave artists were skillful in drawing animals. They stylized the legs, making them very thin in proportion to the body. Many of these have three colors. Sometimes the natural irregularity of the rock face is used by the artist to give the animal additional characteristics. Cave painting is not confined to one particular area; it occurs over much of the world.

Vocabulary

- **Altamira**

  near Santillana del Mar, Cantabria, in Northern Spain

- **Magdalenian culture**

  the last of Upper Paleolithic cultures from 16,000 to 9,000 B.C.

- **ochre**

  a mixture of clay and hydrated iron oxide, ranging in color from light yellow to red and brown; further variations in color are caused by heating

- **oxide**

  a binary compound of oxygen with an element or radical

Dispatch a Cache of Cave Art *(cont.)*

Technique of Cave Artists

Early cave people were not as primitive as previously thought by some historians. Their art reveals an advanced thinking capacity. It is known that they were able to think abstractly on the symbolic level. Looking at European cave art shows that early man used a variety of techniques. They used yellow, red, brown, black, and white pigments. Paint was applied with fingers or crude brushes.

Engraving was also done with different techniques. The rock surface was punctured with a sharp object to create a series of dots; sometimes a fine outline was chiseled. Scratching or scraping was also used.

Suggestions for a Project

Project

Make a cave containing cave art.

Materials Needed

Cave: one brown paper bag (20#) per student, watercolor or thinned tempera paint, 1" (2.5 cm) paintbrush, bowl of water, paper towels

Cave art: book with pictures of cave art, #220 grit (or finer) sandpaper, pencil, eraser, scissors, paste, ruler, crayons, 1/4" (.6 cm) brush, solvent such as lighter fluid or paint thinner. (Note: Extra supervision is needed when using solvent.)

Directions

Cave: Beginning at the opening of the 20# bag, fold back loosely but do not crease about 3" (7.5 cm) at a time until the bag measures about 6" (15 cm) in height. Shape the folds to resemble the mouth of a cave. Using thinned earth colors, paint the bag to look like a cave. Let dry. Add small stalactites made of paper, if desired.

Cave art: Measure the bottom of the paper bag. It should be about 7" x 12" (18 cm x 30 cm). Cut sandpaper to fit the bottom of the bag. Lay bag aside. On the sandpaper, pencil in some animals, superimposing some animals over others. Color with crayon and brush over finished work with a brush dipped sparingly in solvent to make the color blend with the sandpaper. When finished, paste the cave art inside the bottom of the sack. Cave and cave art are complete. (Note: Use only the colors listed in Technique of Cave Artists.)

Dispatch a Cache of Cave Art *(cont.)*

Evaluation: Interpretation of the Artists' Technique

1. Did the student use designated colors?
2. Did the student make animal's legs thin?
3. Did the student brush crayon with solvent?
4. Did the student superimpose some animals?
5. Did the student have variety in picture?

Test Questions

1. How old are Altamira cave paintings?
2. Name two ways cave artists preserved art.
3. Besides paintings, what did cave people leave behind?
4. Name the colors used by cave artists.
5. Is cave painting found only in France and Spain?

Answers to Test Questions

1. Altamira paintings are 10,000–20,000 years old.
2. The artists used pigments from the earth and placed their art deep within the caves.
3. Cave people left behind hearths, tools, and food.
4. Artists used shades of yellow, red, brown, white, and black.
5. Cave painting is found in many parts of the world.

Sample Project

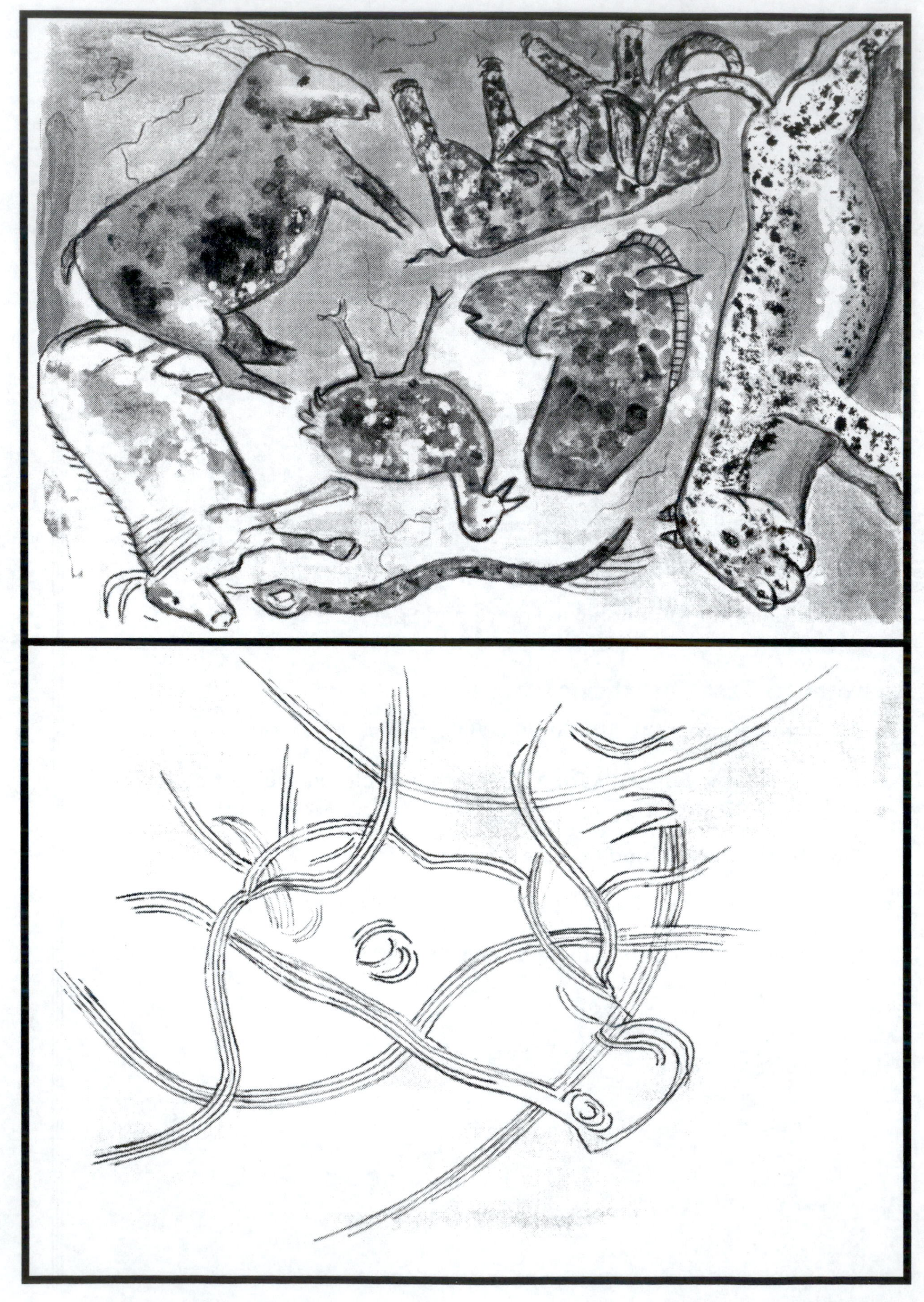

Create Icons of Gold: Relics of Old

The Icon

The icon is a religious painting, usually of God, Jesus, Mary, or a saint. Very little is known of the early artists who painted them. These religious pictures are used in place of statues in some churches of the eastern world. It takes great skill to paint an icon. Many are encrusted with jewels and decorated with gold leaf (gilding).

An icon is both an artistic representation and a spiritual experience for the viewer. It aids the spectator to participate in the divine life of God. The artist who makes an icon is expected to live a life above reproach and to fast and pray in order to convey divine truth through the medium of iconography.

Icons must conform to strict, formal rules. The majority of early icons show a meticulous craftmanship.

Vocabulary

- **icon**
  from the Greek meaning *image*, and in later times it has come to mean *holy image*

- **Byzantium**
  a city in Eastern Greece, later known as Constantinople

- **gold leaf**
  sheets of gold, which were about 1/200,00 of an inch thick—so thin that light shines through it

Create Icons of Gold: Relics of Old *(cont.)*

Technique of the Artists

Byzantine artists were not interested in making their figures look human; they painted them to look otherworldly. The forms are flat and two-dimensional; eyes are dark and shaded; noses long and slender. Brows are arched; faces are heart-shaped with tiny, well-shaped mouths and aesthetic-looking hands. Gold leaf is used extensively. Insets of angels or other figures are also used.

Suggestions for a Project

Project

Using the icon technique, the student draws a person he/she admires and makes a fancy gold frame for it.

Materials Needed

81/2" x 11" (21.5 cm x 28 cm) white construction paper, pencil, eraser, ruler, scissors, paste, colored chalk, markers, lace, gold spray paint, brush, black ballpoint pen, gold paint to brush on, solvent for cleanup, cardboard for frame, colored glass gemstones (available at craft stores), hanger

Directions

Draw the head of a person using the icon technique. Outline with black ballpoint pen. Color picture with chalk and markers. Use gold paint for background, haloes, and trim on garments.

Cut a frame from cardboard. Paste lace on frame. Let dry and spray with gold paint. Paste on glass gemstones. Fit icon into frame and add hanger.

Sample Project

Create Icons of Gold: Relics of Old *(cont.)*

Evaluation: Student Interpretation of the Artist's Technique

1. Does the student's icon look two-dimensional?
2. Are the eyes of the icon large, dark, and shaded?
3. Is the nose long and slender?
4. Is the mouth small and well-shaped?
5. Is the icon colorful? Is gold used generously?
6. Is the face somewhat heart-shaped?
7. Is the frame well made with a generous sprinkling of "gemstones"?

Test Questions

1. What is a religious icon?
2. What subject matter is used for an icon?
3. Where are religious icons generally used?
4. Name three characteristics of an icon.
5. Describe the ornate frames of some icons.
6. Comment on what is expected of an artist who makes an icon.

Answer to Test Questions

1. An icon is a religious painting that must be painted with strict, aesthetic rules.
2. The subject matter is usually a likeness of God, Jesus, Mary, or the saints.
3. Icons are generally used in churches in the East, instead of statues. (*Note*: They are also used in people's homes.)
4. Any of these characteristics are acceptable: large, dark-shaded eyes, strongly arched eyebrows; heart-shaped faces; long, slender hands; small well-shaped mouths; long, slender noses; flat, two-dimensional quality; an otherworldly appearance.
5. The frames of icons are sometimes ornate, gold in color, and often encrusted with jewels.
6. The maker of an icon must be of good character. He is expected to pray and fast while working on the icon.

Draw Wings in Flight: Angelico's Delight

Life of the Artist

Fra Angelico (Brother Angelico) of Fiesole, near Florence, Italy, was a friar in the Dominican Order. In his painting, he expressed traditional ideas and values in religious art.

Around 1440, Angelico painted frescoes in his Florentine Monastery of San Marco. These frescoes, which were painted on wet plaster, are among his most beautiful work. He painted a sacred scene in every monk's cell and at the end of each corridor.

The art of perspective posed no difficulty to Fra Angelico. The paintings depict directness and delicacy, as well as spatial order. Angelico wanted to represent the sacred story in all its beauty and simplicity and subtle relations between human and geometric shapes.

His paintings do not show movement or suggestion of real solid bodies, but have an ethereal quality that is emotionally moving. Angelico did not correct or rework his paintings once they were on the canvas, because he felt he should leave them as they first appeared, believing his talent was a manifestation of God's will. He always prayed before he began his paintings.

Vocabulary

- **frescoes**

  the art of painting on a wall, on freshly spread, moist lime plaster, using color pigments in a water base

- **perspective**

  the spatial relation of objects, as they appear to the eye

- **simplicity**

  directness of expression, plainness

Draw Wings in Flight: Angelico's Delight *(cont.)*

Technique of the Artist

Fra Angelico painted frescoes on damp plaster, using soft pastels, which blended into darker shades of the same color. His figures were often framed in Romanesque arches or Gothic vaults. The angels' wings were patterned and decorative; the haloes around the heads of the saint appeared to be fluted and painted with gold leaf. His figures were delicately drawn and diffused with gentle light.

Suggestions for a Project

Project

Students will draw a guardian angel or a scene with angels.

Materials Needed

9" x 12" (23 cm x 30 cm) white construction paper, colored chalk, pencil, eraser, gold paint, black pinpoint marker, old Christmas cards, religious magazines, fixative or super-hold hair spray

Directions

Using religious magazines or old Christmas cards, find pictures of angels for the students to use for ideas. Ask the students to draw a composition with angels and then color the pictures using colored chalk. Have students outline with fine marker to emphasize details. Spray with super-hold hair spray, which will act as a fixative, to make the chalk permanent.

Draw Wings in Flight: Angelico's Delight *(cont.)*

Evaluation: Student Interpretation of the Artist's Technique

1. Did the student blend pastels to give a three-dimensional effect?
2. Did the student use soft colors?
3. Did the student frame the composition with geometric forms?
4. Did the student make the angel's wings decorative?
5. Did the student make gold, patterned haloes?

Test Questions

1. From what country did Fra Angelico come?
2. What type of art did Fra Angelico prefer to do?
3. Define the meaning of *fresco*.
4. Did Fra Angelico's paintings have any special qualities?
5. Did Fra Angelico's paintings show movement?

Answers to Test Questions

1. Fra Angelico came from Italy.
2. Fra Angelico liked to do frescoes.
3. *Fresco* is the art of painting on plaster that is still damp, using water-based paints.
4. Fra Angelico's paintings seemed to be otherworldly, rather weightless, and ethereal.
5. Fra Angelico's paintings usually did not show movement. They had a rather static quality.

Sample Project

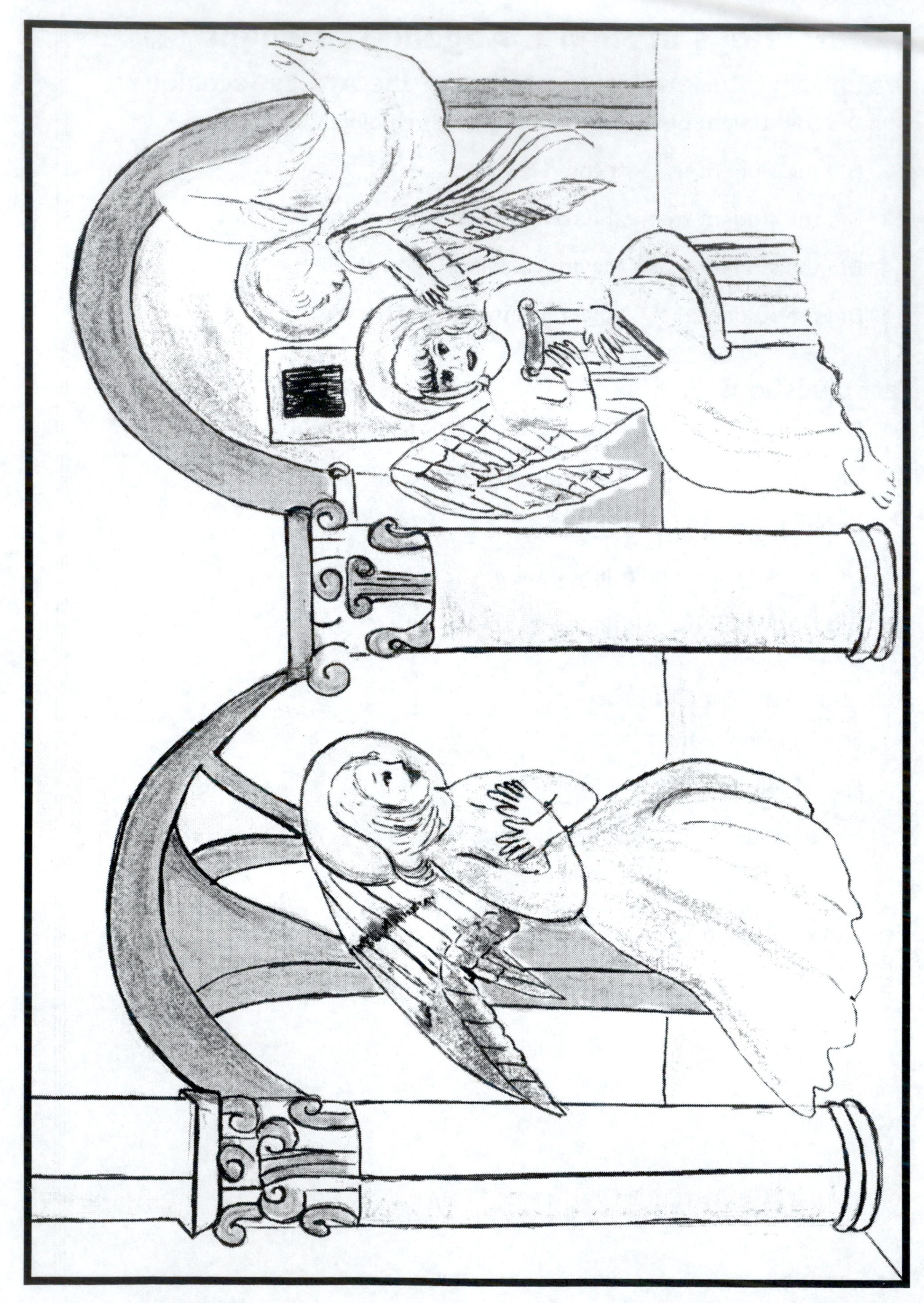

Compose Colorful Celebrations with Bruegel

Life of the Artist

The year and the place of Bruegel's birth are in doubt, but it is thought to be between 1525 and 1530. Some authorities believe he may have been born in Belgium, possibly in the province of Brabant. In 1563, he married Mayken, the daughter of artist Pieter Coecke van Aelst. They were married at Easter time, and soon his mother-in-law insisted the couple move to Brussels. Most of his career was spent in Antwerp and Brussels. Three of his sons were also artists: Pieter the younger, Jan, and Ambrose, but none attained the remarkable skill of their father. He was an artistic genius who loved to paint the everyday life of peasants. He also painted many beautiful landscapes.

One of his well-known paintings, *The Wedding Dance*, hangs in the Detroit Institute of Arts. A trip to Rome and other cities helped him to find breathtaking landscapes, which he sketched and brought back to his studio.

In Brussels he found new patrons, including Cardinal de Granvelle, Archbishop of Mechelen, and Phillip II who owned several of his works. One famous one owned by Phillip II was *Landscape with Flight into Egypt*. Bruegel died in 1569.

Vocabulary

- **landscape**
  a picture representing a view of landforms and scenery
- **etching**
  the art of producing pictures or designs by first inking and printing from a metal, wooden, linoleum, or other material plate incised with a design
- **Realist**
  an artist who draws pictures which are true-to-life, without idealizing the forms

Compose Colorful Celebrations with Bruegel

(cont.)

Technique of the Artist

Bruegel painted in clear, flat colors without the use of shadows. His paintings show a remarkable balance that is very delicately achieved. His perspective is superb. Bruegel's drawings, paintings, and prints express a theme, which conveys humility and tolerance, especially in his depictions of peasants and their festivities. Bruegel was a Realist.

Suggestions for a Project

Project

Students may select a holiday or event that calls for a celebration and draw it on paper. The scene may be modern or historical. Students will use Bruegel's technique to complete the picture.

Materials Needed

12" x 18" (30 cm x 46 cm) white drawing paper, pencil, eraser, ruler, tempera paint, brushes, paper towels, bowl of water, polymer medium (optional), fluorescent paint for highlights, contrasting construction paper, scissors, glue

Directions

Sketch a holiday or other celebratory event on white drawing paper. Use bright, flat colors of paint in the technique of Pieter Bruegel. If desired, the florescent paint can be used to add a festive touch to the holiday events.

After the paint is thoroughly dry, brush the entire composition with matte-type polymer. Allow composition to dry thoroughly. Frame or mount composition with contrasting construction paper.

Compose Colorful Celebrations with Bruegel *(cont.)*

Evaluation: Student Interpretation of the Artist's Technique

1. Did the student use clear, flat colors?
2. Did the holiday event have a festive appearance?
3. Are the forms of the composition balanced?
4. Does the composition express a theme?
5. Does the composition have a realistic quality?

Test Questions

1. What were two of Bruegel's favorite subjects to paint?
2. Describe Bruegel's painting technique.
3. Name a well-known painting by Bruegel.
4. Why is Bruegel classed as a Realist?
5. Do Bruegel's paintings tell a story? Explain your answer with proof.

Answers to Test Questions

1. Bruegel liked to paint landscapes and peasant life.
2. Bruegel painted in clear, flat colors without the use of shadows. He painted rather large, panoramic views with skillful perspective. His paintings usually had a very obvious theme.
3. Students may name *The Wedding Dance*, *Landscape with Flight into Egypt*, or any other famous painting by Bruegel.
4. Bruegel is classed as a Realist because he drew and painted his figures true-to-life without any stylization.
5. Many of Bruegel's paintings tell a story. They have a definite theme and are so graphic that it is not difficult to discern the meaning of Bruegel's work, for example, *The Wedding Dance*.

Sample Project

Generate Weather Scenes with El Greco

Life of the Artist

El Greco was born in Iraklion, Crete, in 1541. He was considered one of the world's greatest mannerist painters, because of his ability to absorb and apply the techniques of masters such as Titian, Tintoretto, and other great artists. His given name was Domenikos Theotokopoulos, but he was known by the nickname "El Greco."

An excellent draftsman, he combined court elegance in his emphasis of religious fervor. The saints in his paintings were figments of ghostly imagination. The portraits he painted were life-like.

It is thought that he may have studied Byzantine art in his native land of Crete before studying with Tintoretto and other masters, where he learned the style of painting called mannerism. This technique employs graceful lines, elongated and somewhat abstract forms, and colors with a metallic appearance coupled with white highlights.

El Greco traveled to Rome and to Toledo looking for patronage. He did not gain favor because King Philip did not like his painting, *The Martyrdom of St. Maurice*. He greatly influenced the Impressionists many years later with his painting entitled *Laocoon*, which inspired the viewer with deep emotion. He died in 1614.

Vocabulary

- **highlights**

  any surface in an art piece which catches the most light

- **baroque**

  an artistic style characterized by elaborate, ornate, and sometimes grotesque forms

- **El Greco**

  a nickname for Domenikos Theotokopoulos, meaning *the Greek*

- **mannerism**

  a style of painting utilizing affected poses along with grouping and lighting effects; It also has graceful lines, elongated, semi-abstract forms, and slightly metallic colors with white highlights

Generate Weather Scenes with El Greco *(cont.)*

Technique of the Artist

His paintings from 1600 to 1614 were Baroque. After that, he emphasized the distortion of space, light, and form in the mannerist style. In his maturity, he became a master of portraiture, employing dazzling color, realistic texture, and skillful foreshortening.

Suggestions for a Project

Project

Students will use El Greco's technique to create a series of four pictures depicting the seasons of spring, summer, fall, and winter. They will use strong contrasts and interesting textures.

Materials Needed

a selection of several colors of 9" x 12" (23 cm x 30 cm) construction paper suitable for backgrounds; a variety of mediums from which students may choose—Polymer medium, tempera, water pan, brushes, paper towels, white or colored chalk, white glitter, newspaper, all purpose glue (dried clear), paint palette; spray fixative or super-hold hairspray; corrugated cardboard; string (Note to teacher: Students may use any other material needed to help them achieve texture in their compositions.)

Directions

Ask students to divide the color of construction paper they have chosen into four equal parts and sketch a season on each part. Perhaps the student will sketch a spring rain. Polymer medium used very thick will make excellent raindrops when dry. White glitter will add interest to winter scenes. Ask the students to use sharp contrasts in color, as El Greco did. The white or colored chalk will help to add extra highlights when their paintings are dry. Watered paint with polymer medium added will give a glistening effect. Mount on corrugated, cardboard the same size as the picture. Add string hangers.

Generate Weather Scenes with El Greco *(cont.)*

Evaluation: Student Interpretation of the Artist's Technique

1. Did the student draw meaningful and realistic scenes?
2. Did the student use textures wisely?
3. Do the pictures show strong contrasts as in El Greco's painting?
4. Are the highlights on the pictures well located?
5. Is the overall arrangement attractive?

Test Questions

1. Why was the artist called "El Greco"?
2. What style did El Greco use in his painting?
3. What famous painting of El Greco's greatly influenced the impressionists?
4. Why was El Greco considered one of the greatest mannerist painters of his time?
5. What style was El Greco's paintings from 1600 to 1614?

Answers to Test Questions

1. El Greco did most of his painting in Spain, but because his native land was Greece, he was called "El Greco," the Greek.
2. For most of his life, El Greco used the mannerist style of painting.
3. The painting was entitled *Laocoon*.
4. He was considered the greatest mannerist painter of his time because of his ability to absorb the skills of artists such as Titian, Tintoretto, and other masters.
5. His paintings were done in the Baroque style.

Sample Project

An Art Venture with Velasquez

Life of the Artist

Diego Velasquez was born in Seville, Spain, June 6, 1599. He painted in the same style as Caravaggio, but his work also shows some of the influences of Zurbaran. His subject matter was portraits and still life.

He was appointed court painter to Philip IV in Madrid, Spain, where he spent the rest of his life painting portraits of the royal family. He painted scenes from everyday life (genre) as well as landscape, mythological, and religious paintings.

Velasquez used a division of light and shade with clear outlines in the early period of his work. In the late 1620s, his work began to change and a new richness was seen in his paintings. Most of Velasquez's works are royal portraits with specific set patterns.

He also did paintings that were entirely his own creation. One of these is the well-known *Maids of Honor* of 1656 in which he was preoccupied with the effect of light, a contributing factor to its greatness and his popularity throughout the succeeding centuries. Velasquez died in Madrid on August 6, 1660.

Vocabulary

- **portrait**
  a pictorial representation of a person, usually of the head
- **baroque**
  a style of artistic expression which is ornate with colors changing from warm to cool and the texture changing from crisp to soft
- **light pattern**
  the relationship of light and dark shades appearing on a form, due to its physical features and the direction of the light striking it
- **surface quality**
  the visual and tactile character of an object; its texture

An Art Venture with Velasquez *(cont.)*

Technique of the Artist

Velasquez was greatly influenced by Titian and Rubens. He used light to create interest. His light treatment was original and very arresting to the viewer because his technique enhanced both color and form, with its subtle varieties and nuances.

He was also influenced by Caravaggio and learned to limit his colors. Sometimes he used only black and neutrals. His brush strokes were short or long and thin, sometimes thick, and this gave the viewer the impression that his technique was carefree and spontaneous, but it was in fact, very calculated and well-planned.

Velasquez succeeded in capturing the essence of what he painted, rather than trying to catch every detail. He was known as the "painter's painter."

Suggestions for a Project

Project 1

Students will explore texture by using crayons to make rubbings of various textures such as raised patterns on wallpaper samples, materials with a raised texture, or stones with engraved sections. When students have collected a variety of textures, they will cut out shapes to create a portrait or a still life. They will use light to give a three-dimensional effect.

Materials Needed

wallpaper sample books, old lace, materials, ruler, crayons, construction paper, glue, scissors, pencil

Directions

Collect a variety of textures from rubbings. Cut out needed shapes and paste on construction paper.

Project 2

Students will draw a self-portrait or select a friend and paint a portrait of that person. They should use light in their portraits.

Materials Needed

white drawing paper, pencil, acrylic or watercolor paint, brushes, water cup and water, paper towels, contrasting paper, glue or paste

Directions

Sketch a portrait lightly on drawing paper. Paint with acrylic paint or watercolor. Mount on contrasting paper.

An Art Venture with Velasquez *(cont.)*

Evaluation: Student Interpretation of the Artist's Technique

1. Did the student use light to make the composition look three-dimensional?
2. Did the student capture the essence of the composition?
3. Did the student use a variety of textures?
4. Were the forms well proportioned?
5. Was the negative space used creatively?

Test Questions

1. What kind of art did Velasquez do most of his lifetime?
2. Name other types of art Velasquez did.
3. What technique made Velasquez's work outstanding?
4. What painting is Velasquez noted for?
5. What was Velasquez's native country?

Answers to Test Questions

1. Velasquez painted portraits for royalty most of his lifetime.
2. Velasquez also painted landscape, mythological, and religious scenes and scenes from everyday life.
3. Velasquez treated light in innovative ways.
4. Velasquez is especially noted for his painting, *Maids of Honor*.
5. Velasquez's native country was Spain.

Sample Project

On the Burner with Turner

Life of the Artist

Joseph Mallord William Turner was born in London on April 23, 1775. While he was still a teenager, he was privileged to exhibit his paintings at the Royal Academy of Arts, where he also received his art education, beginning at age fourteen. Later he became a professor and full member of the Royal Academy.

Turner, like Caravaggio in an earlier century, was known for the way he treated light in his paintings, especially in his landscapes and seascapes. He also illustrated poems and learned the art of engraving. His favored medium was watercolor until late in the last decade of the 1700s when he began to use oil paint.

As a young man, he liked to paint historical and mythological scenes, which had misty, atmospheric effects. About 1820, his painting became more colorful as he began to use brighter shades of paint and to diffuse light more skillfully. By 1835, when Turner was about 60 years old, the subjects of his paintings merged with the atmosphere and became indistinct through a colorful haze. His most masterful painting was during this period.

Turner's work with light was very important as a prelude to the development of impressionism, because he showed the impressionists one way of capturing light with paint. Turner died in London on December 19, 1857.

Vocabulary

- **diffuse**

  to break up and distribute by reflection (as light)

- **medium**

  a material or technical means of expression

- **Caravaggio**

  Michelangelo Merisi (1571–1610) from the town of Caravaggio near Milan; He adopted the town's name as his own.

On the Burner with Turner *(cont.)*

Technique of the Artist

Turner planned his paintings to achieve diffused light. He began with a light yellow wash and added small areas of red and blue mixed slightly into yellow. When dry, he indicated his composition with chalk. He then laid in large areas with thick white and color. After drying, he added details with a light shade of brown. Color glazes of various intensities and white completed the picture. A final finishing glaze was added.

Suggestions for a Project

Project

Draw a Fourth of July fireworks display.

Materials Needed

12″ x 18″ (30 cm x 46 cm) medium blue construction paper, 12″ x 18″ (30 cm x 46 cm) dark blue construction paper, scraps of yellow or orange construction paper, pencil, eraser, scissors, brushes, fluorescent-type paints, silver glitter, glue, white tempera, book with pictures of fireworks displays, black permanent marker, black ballpoint pen

Directions

Cut a 4″ x 18″ (10 cm x 46 cm) strip of dark blue construction paper. Paste it to the bottom of the medium blue paper. Sketch with pencil a skyline with outlines of trees and mountains in the distance. Draw human figures looking towards the sky. Outline pencil drawings with black ballpoint pen and fill in figures, trees, and mountains with black marker to give a silhouette effect. From yellow or orange construction paper, cut a small moon to paste in the sky. Add a few wispy clouds with thinned white tempera.

Lightly pencil in a fireworks display. Color with bright colors of fluorescent-type paint. When dry, apply a thin line of glue to the display. Sprinkle silver glitter in the glue. Shake off excess glitter. Frame with remaining dark blue paper cut into strips.

On the Burner with Turner *(cont.)*

Evaluation: Student Interpretation of the Artist's Technique

1. Did the student make a carefully designed skyline?
2. Is the night sky well composed?
3. Do the fireworks displays have interesting colors and patterns?
4. Does the landscape add believable accents to the picture?
5. Is the overall picture well planned and attractive?

Test Questions

1. What was the outstanding feature of J. M. W. Turner's paintings?
2. What important effect did Turner's technique have on the development of impressionism?
3. When did Turner do his most masterful work?
4. How are Caravaggio and Turner alike?
5. What was Turner's favorite kind of paint in his younger years? When he was an older artist?

Answers to Test Questions

1. Turner was noted for the way he painted light into his pictures.
2. Turner showed the Impressionists one way to paint light into a picture.
3. Turner did his best work when he was about 60 years old.
4. Caravaggio and Turner both liked to capture light in their paintings.
5. Turner liked to use watercolor when he was young; when he was older he began to use oil paint.

Sample Project

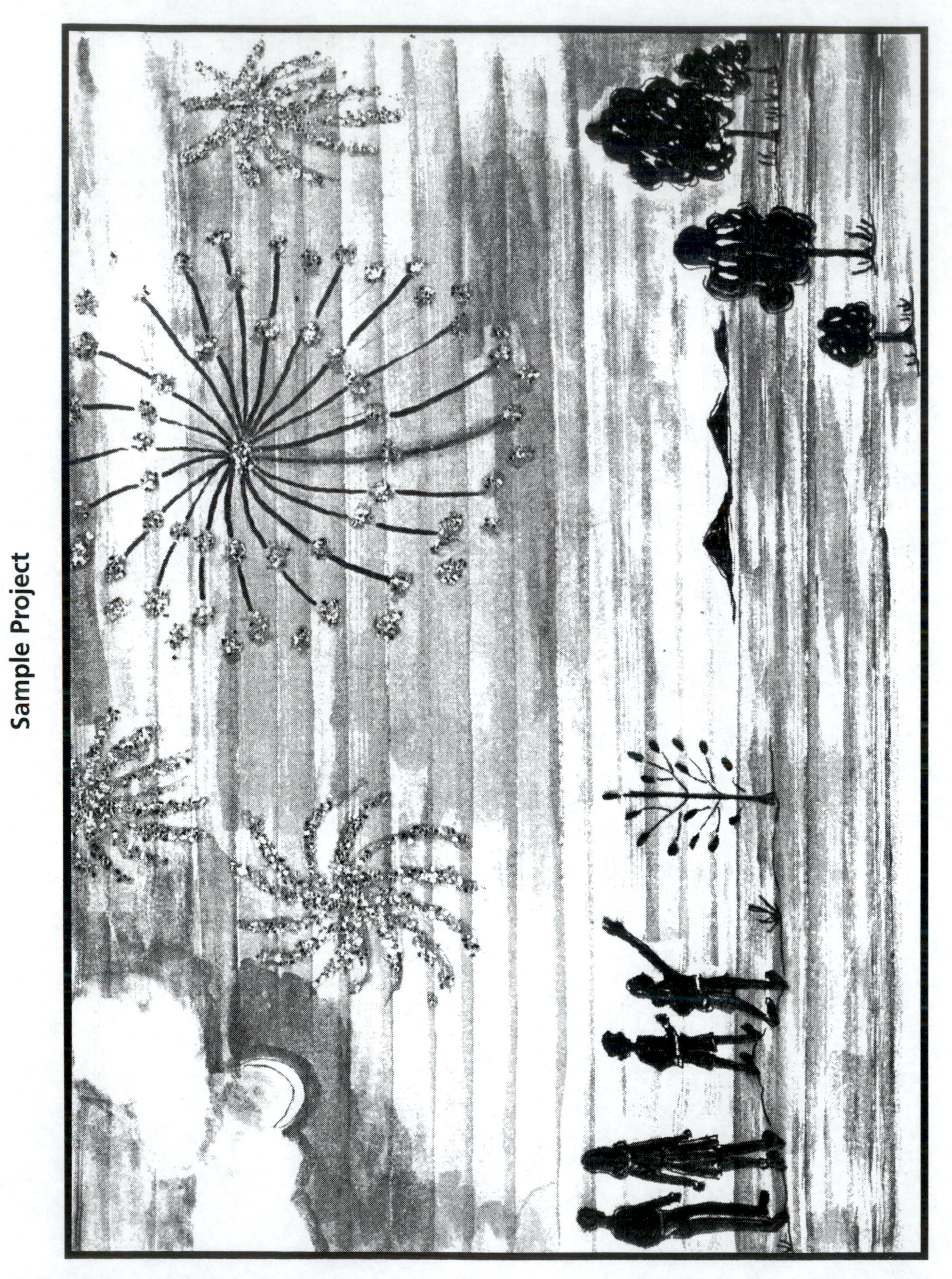

Make an Archaic Mosaic

Life of the Artist

Gioacchino Barberi was born in 1783. He was among the first artists to produce miniature mosaics, which were inspired by paintings at Herculaneum, Italy. He was interested in art, particularly mosaics. He made very delicate mosaics, some of which were only 2¾" x 2" (7 cm x 5 cm). He invented black glass tesserae to bring out the beauty of the forms he designed, in imitation of the paintings of Herculaneum.

Vocabulary

- **mosaic**

  a surface decoration made by inlaying small pieces of colored material to form pictures or patterns

- **tesserae**

  small flat pieces of marble, glass, or tile used in mosaic work

- **Herculaneum**

  a city near Pompeii in Italy that was buried under volcanic ash when Mount Vesuvius erupted in 79 A.D.

- **working sketch**

  a plan drawn to guide the artist in making a mosaic

Make an Archaic Mosaic *(cont.)*

Technique of the Artist

Gioacchino Barberi liked to work with miniatures. It was necessary for him to make a working sketch along with a plan for the type of colored stones he would need to complete his pictures. Colored and shaded tesserae were sorted into separate containers. A thin coat of mortar was applied to the chosen surface.

The working sketch was laid over the damp mortar. The lines from the sketch were etched on the mortar. The tesserae were then placed in the mortar and allowed to dry. Transferable ink may be used in place of the etching and a glaze added after it dries.

Suggestions for a Project

Project

Make a mosaic, using colors cut from old magazine pictures.

Materials Needed

9" x 12" (23 cm x 30 cm) white drawing paper, scissors, paste, egg carton, old magazines, pencil, eraser, construction paper for frame, clear plastic spray

Directions

Draw a working sketch of a simple scene with large areas of color. Designate on the sketch the colors to be used. From old magazines, cut out areas of color. Cut each color into small pieces to be used for tesserae. Separate each color into a compartment of an egg carton. Paste tesserae in designated places until entire picture is covered. Do not overlap tesserae. Leave a fine line of space between each tesserae. Cut dark-colored tesserae for the background. When mosaic is entirely dry, the student or teacher may give it a light plastic coating. Frame with construction paper.

Make an Archaic Mosaic *(cont.)*

Evaluation: Student Interpretation of the Artist's Technique

1. Did the student make a working sketch of the mosaic?
2. Did the student use a dark background?
3. Is the student's composition well defined?
4. Are tesserae pasted carefully without protruding corners or overlapping?
5. Is the finished composition attractive?

Test Questions

1. What type of mosaics did Barberi prefer to make?
2. What did Barberi invent?
3. Why did Barberi need to invent what he did?
4. Describe the steps in making a mosaic.
5. For what reason is a working sketch important in making a mosaic?

Answers to Test Questions

1. Barberi preferred to make miniature mosaics.
2. Barberi invented black glass tesserae.
3. Barberi used the black glass tesserae to enhance the forms he designed.
4. A working sketch is made. A thick coat of mortar is applied to the surface designated for the mosaic. The working sketch is etched in to the mortar, then tesserae are placed in the mortar and allowed to dry.
5. A working sketch guides the artist to make a well defined mosaic.

Sample Project

Plot a Portrait with Morisot

Life of the Artist

Berthe Morisot was born in France January 14, 1841. She was the daughter of an important government official and the granddaughter of the famous painter, Fragonard. She was also the sister-in-law of Edouard Manet. She had many artist relatives of distinction. She married Edouard's brother Eugene in 1874, and their home became a gathering place for the impressionists.

She was given painting lessons and developed a style distinctively impressionistic. She influenced the painting technique of Manet, even encouraging him to paint outdoors. After famous painters such as Renoir and others had abandoned the movement, she continued with the Impressionistic style. Besides painting, she posed for many of Manet's paintings.

Unlike her sister Edma, who gave up painting after her marriage, Berthe made painting a career. She is considered one of the most important women painters of the nineteenth century, producing over 350 works of art.

On March 2, 1895, at the age of 54, Berthe died of pneumonia. She willed some of her works to famous artists such as Degas, Renoir, and Monet.

Vocabulary

- **iridescent quality**

  a production of glistening rainbow colors

- **genre scenes**

  a style of painting depicting everyday life

- **pearlized paint**

  paints available in many stores that have the softly glowing quality of real pearls

- **French impressionism**

  The impressionists challenged traditional ideas about art and style. Sunlight was broken down into its component parts. They achieved this by laying small layers of color in close proximity, to be mixed by the eye. This was a new way of visual representation.

Plot a Portrait with Morisot *(cont.)*

Technique of the Artist

Berthe worked both in oil and watercolor. She painted many genre scenes and landscapes. Her pictures have an atmospheric intimacy and an iridescent quality, which she achieved by applying freely large touches of paint. Her works have freshness and a new way of seeing and depicting her world.

Suggestions for a Project

Project

The students will do a self-portrait, genre scene, or landscape of the 1800s. Care should be taken to research thoroughly the fashions of the day as well as the inventions of that time.

Materials Needed

book on fashions of the 1800s; genre scenes of the 1800s; pearlized, water-based paint; glue; 11" x 14" (28 cm x 36 cm) black construction paper; brushes; cup of water; paper towels; pencil; eraser; large, gray construction paper for a frame; scissors; ruler

Directions

Sketch the subject of choice on the black paper. Ask students to pay special attention to the colors used. Morisot's colors were muted. To achieve this technique, students may have to mix white, pearlized paint with other colors to soften the color to a tint, as Morisot did. Be sure the students blend the colors well so the paint does not look too bright nor too watery. When painting is finished, mount on gray construction paper.

Plot a Portrait with Morisot *(cont.)*

Evaluation: Student Interpretation of the Artist's Technique

1. Did the student choose an appropriate theme for the painting?
2. Did the student use the pearlized paint effectively?
3. Did the student use large touches of paint freely?
4. Did the finished painting have an iridescent quality?
5. Does the student's technique resemble the technique of Berthe Morisot?

Test Questions

1. Why do you think Berthe Morisot is considered one of the most important female painters of the nineteenth century?
2. What technique did Berthe Morisot choose to use for her paintings?
3. Did Berthe Morisot continue to paint in this style after some well-known artists had abandoned it?
4. How did Berthe Morisot influence the work of Manet?
5. Explain the meaning of *genre scene*.

Answers to Test Questions

1. Berthe Morisot is considered one of the most important of the women painters of the nineteenth century because of her skill in drawing and her outstanding talent in applying paint.
2. Berthe Morisot used the technique of the impressionists.
3. Berthe Morisot continued to paint in the style of the impressionists after other artists had abandoned it.
4. She encouraged Manet to adopt the style of the impressionists and to paint outdoors.
5. *Genre scene* means a scene from everyday life.

Sample Project

Natural Flow with Vincent Van Gogh

Life of the Artist

Vincent Van Gogh was born on March 30, 1853, in the Netherlands. He was the son of a minister, and tried becoming a minister himself, but he failed. He also failed at becoming an art dealer, so he entered the Academy of Art in Brussels, to learn to be a painter. He left the academy and decided to teach himself to draw and paint. Most of his life he was supported by his younger brother, Theo.

Van Gogh was greatly affected by his exposure to the brilliant coloring of impressionism. He began to make thick linear strokes of rhythmic and symbolic lines which gave movement to the surface of his paintings.

Vincent painted 600 paintings during his lifetime and he sold only one, but today his paintings are worth millions of dollars. His life ended tragically in 1890 when Vincent was 37 years old.

Vocabulary

- **rhythmic**

  movement of fluctuation marked by the recurrence of natural flow of related elements

- **symbolic**

  exalting the mysterious and mystical elements, and unifying the arts and functions of the senses

- **impressionism**

  a style of painting created by a group of French artists about 1879, depicting objects by means of dabs or strokes of unmixed colors to simulate reflected light

Natural Flow with Vincent Van Gogh *(cont.)*

Technique of Van Gogh

Van Gogh created paintings full of stong emotion, vibrant colors, and images that seemed to wiggle and vibrate. He sculpted with paint, putting the paint thickly in his canvas, and sometimes squeezing paint directly from the tube onto the canvas. He achieved interesting texture by using thick and thin lines, forming them with skillful use of his brush.

Suggestions for a Project

Project 1

Sketch a land or seascape outdoors or use a photo or clip interesting scenery from a magazine. Use Van Gogh's technique for the picture.

Materials Needed

9" x 12" (23 cm x 30 cm) white drawing paper, pencil, eraser, oil crayon, tissues

Directions

Sketch scene lightly, correcting for proportion and detail. Use a pencil to add thick and thin lines as a guide to create texture. Ask students to begin coloring at the top of the page and work to the bottom. Oil crayons have a tendency to smear. If mixing colors is desired, oils can be mixed with fingers or a tissue.

Project 2

Students may wish to sketch a picture of their room, as Van Gogh did in *Bedroom at Aries.*

Materials Needed

Heavy cardboard (cut from boxes), pencil, eraser, electric food warming tray, hot pads, small tins for melting crayons, old or broken crayons, small paint brush, good solvent for cleaning up wax drippings

Directions

Sketch the scene lightly on cardboard. Melt crayons in muffin or other small tins on warming tray. Brush on melted crayon. Crayon will crack and flake if cardboard is not firm. Apply heavy and light lines to similar Van Gogh's technique. Note to teacher: You will need extra helpers to supervise this project.

Natural Flow with Vincent Van Gogh *(cont.)*

Evaluation: Interpretation of Artist's Technique

1. Did the student use lines to create motion?
2. Did the student use vibrant colors?
3. Did the student achieve a good texture?
4. Did the student use nature or genre to create the composition?
5. Did the student include thick and think lines?

Test Questions

1. What "ism" in the art world influenced Van Gogh?
2. Explain the phrase, "Van Gogh sculpted with paint."
3. How did Van Gogh achieve rhythm in his painting?
4. Was Van Gogh successful as an artist during his lifetime?
5. Comment on Van Gogh's success as an artist today.

Answers to Test Questions

1. Van Gogh was influenced by impressionism.
2. Van Gogh used paint thickly, giving his paintings a built-up texture.
3. He repeated lines and forms rhythmically.
4. Van Gogh sold only one painting in his lifetime.
5. Today Van Gogh's paintings are worth millions of dollars.

Sample Project

Painting Dots with Georges Seurat

Life of the Artist

Georges Seurat was born in Paris, France, in 1859. He was known as Post-Impressionist and also as a Neo-Impressionist because he developed a new system of painting known as pointillism. He used the color theories of French physicist, Eugene Chevreul. He was concerned with light, shadow, and color. Seurat devised a system of semi-uniform dots juxtaposed, so that at a distance the colors mixed in the eye of the viewer. It took a great deal of time and skill to achieve the remarkable gradation of light and shadow as well as exquisite color and form in his paintings.

Seurat was strongly influenced by the works of Claude Monet and Camille Pissarro, who applied their colors in delicate layers. The three men were fascinated with color theory, but it was Seurat who developed a more controlled and scientific approach to translating color theory into a workable painting technique.

Seurat painted almost constantly, but he completed few works because of the time it took to apply the dots. His masterpiece, *Sunday Afternoon on the Island of La Grande Jatte* is very large, almost 7' x 10' (2m x 3m). It took years to complete, and may be seen today at the Art Institute of Chicago. Seurat's technique attracted several artists to pointillism. Seurat died of diptheria at the age of 32 in Paris, where he had lived his entire life.

Vocabulary

- **pointillism**

  a series of dots of pure color, juxtaposed scientifically to be mixed with the eye at a distance

- **La Grande Jatte**

  an island near Paris where people go to enjoy an outing

Painting Dots with Georges Seurat *(cont.)*

Technique of the Artist

Seurat studied the scientific approach to color with its many nuances and devised a system to capture light, shadow and shades of color by juxtaposing dots of pure color, scientifically placed to achieve the effects he desired to make his paintings outstanding.

Seurat's rendition of pictures is extremely complex. He wished to capture the natural world in all its fullness. Each element of Seurat's paintings is filled with nuances of quality and inventiveness.

Suggestions for a Project

Project

Ask the students to select a subject for a composition such as a scene from the circus, from outdoors, or a famous happening or landmark.

Materials Needed

9" x 12" (23 cm x 30 cm) white drawing paper, correction pen, a selection of books and brochures with pictures of the scenes suggested in the project suggestions above, pencil, eraser, a large selection of markers

Directions

Draw a picture of one of the subject matters listed above. Ask the students to fill in the composition using dots placed side by side. Be sure the students understand that they should achieve light and shadow, as well as shades in their compositions as Seurat did. They may use correction pens for errors. (*Note to the teacher*: You will need a large supply of markers for this project. Acrylic or tempera paint may also be used with a fine brush if markers are not available. This project needs careful planning and should be emphasized to the student.)

Painting Dots with Georges Seurat *(cont.)*

Evaluation: Interpretation of the Artist's Technique

1. Did the student stay within the selected subject area?
2. Is the picture well planned and neat in appearance?
3. Does the picture show shaded areas?
4. Does the picture show sunlight areas?
5. Are the dots reasonably uniform so that the colors mix at a distance? (Example: Red and blue dots appear purple.)

Test Questions

1. Explain the meaning of the term *pointillism*.
2. Who was responsible for the scientific theory that helped Seurat develop his technique with color and light?
3. Who were two artists who had an influence on Seurat's work?
4. Why did Seurat paint so few paintings in his career as an artist?
5. What was the name of Seurat's masterpiece?

Answers to Test Questions

1. *Pointillism* is a technique developed by Georges Seurat, consisting of thousands of tiny dots of color placed side by side which supposedly mix as the viewer looks at the painting.
2. Eugene Chevreul developed the color theory Seurat used to develop pointillism.
3. Two artists who influenced Seurat's work were Claude Monet and Camille Pissarro.
4. Seurat's technique took much time to complete and he died when he was very young.
5. The name of Seurat's masterpiece was *Sunday Afternoon on the Island of La Grande Jatte*.

Sample Project

Ponder Grandma Moses: Pretty Primitive

Life of the Artist

Grandma Moses was born September 7, 1860. Her name was Anna Mary Robertson. Grandma Moses liked to draw and paint when she was a child, but she didn't start painting seriously until she was in her seventies. She got her nickname, Grandma Moses, because she was old enough to be a grandma. In January of 1941, she had her first one-artist show.

She made yarn pictures first, then she painted on tree lichens and ceramic tiles, and finally on canvas. She didn't paint when she was young. She married Thomas Salmon Moses in 1887, and became the mother of ten children.

During her lifetime, she painted more than 1,500 pictures, many of which were landscapes. She received an art award from President Harry Truman.

Grandma Moses' style of painting was called American Primitive. She died on December 13, 1961, at the age of 101.

Vocabulary

- **ceramic tile**

  tiles made of clay and baked in a kiln, then painted with a glaze and re-fired

- **landscape**

  a picture representing a view of natural inland scenery

- **one-artist show**

  a work of art usually produced by a self-taught artist

- **tree mushrooms**

  a lichen that grows from the side of a tree like a shelf

Ponder Grandma Moses: Pretty Primitive

(cont.)

Technique of the Artist

Grandma Moses liked to paint simple scenes of everyday life. She painted the farm where she lived in all the different seasons. She showed people making maple syrup, making apple butter, quilting, observing, attending the country fair, and sleigh riding. Most of her pictures showed outdoor scenes, but some were painted inside her house, too. The paintings were very colorful.

Suggestions for a Project

Project

Ask the students to make their own indoor or outdoor scene. They probably don't catch turkeys or make maple syrup, but they do play outdoor games, go on picnics, roller-skate, and have friends over. Or, they can just draw themselves in their own room. They will draw a scene from their own life as Grandma Moses did.

Materials Needed

white drawing paper, colored chalk, marker, black ballpoint pen, super-hold hair spray or fixative, pencil, paper, ruler, colored construction paper

Directions

With a pencil, student sketches a scene from his/her daily life. When it is the way the student wants it, he/she outlines it with a black ballpoint pen. Forms are colored with marker. The background, sky, grass, etc., can be drawn in with chalk. Spray lightly with hairspray to fix chalk areas permanently. Picture may be framed with construction paper.

Ponder Grandma Moses: Pretty Primitive *(cont.)*

Evaluation: Student Interpretation of the Artist's Technique

1. Was American Primitive depicted in the work?
2. Did the student choose an everyday life theme?
3. Did the student use repetitive forms?
4. Was student's composition colorful?
5. Name scenes Grandma used for her paintings.

Test Questions

1. What does the term *American Primitive* mean?
2. Why didn't Grandma Moses paint when she was young?
3. Name materials she used to paint on.
4. What subject matter did she often use?
5. Name scenes Grandma used for her paintings.

Answers to Test Questions

1. *American Primitive* refers to self-taught artists who paint with naïve directness.
2. Grandma Moses had ten children to care for.
3. She painted on tiles, tree lichens, and canvas.
4. The subject Grandma Moses used most was landscapes. She liked outdoor scenes.
5. Other subject matter Grandma Moses used included making apple butter, making maple syrup, quilting, holiday observances, scenes from the country fair, and sleigh riding as well as many other everyday subjects.

Sample Project

Render a Clown with Rouault

Life of the Artist

Georges Rouault was born in Paris, France, in 1871. The son of a cabinet maker, he was sent to a strict, stern, Protestant school, but left at the age of 14 to begin an apprenticeship as a stained glass craftsman. He attended art school at night until 1895. He used his artwork to express his ideas about poverty, war, injustice, and corruption. He was one of the few modern artists to use art as a means to relate his feelings and values.

An intense perfectionist, Rouault destroyed over 300 pieces of artwork that he considered inadequate and flawed. The last ten years of his life was spent trying to reach the goals of perfection he set for himself. He died in 1958.

Vocabulary

- **stained glass**

  a painting done with small pieces of colored glass, cut to shape, and fitted together with lead frames. The glass is then assembled into a stained glass window.

- **expressionism**

  a style of art that shows an expression of personal feelings and emotions

- **impasto**

  the thick application of paint to a canvas or panel in painting

Render a Clown with Rouault *(cont.)*

Technique of the Artist

Rouault was unique among French painters. He used expressionism in his paintings, creating rich impasto and violent strokes with his paintbrush. He was influenced by the stained glass windows he made. His paintings show deep sadness and pity.

Rouault loved medieval art and the glowing colors of stained glass, outlined and defined with black borders.

Suggestions for a Project

Show students various pictures of clowns. Discuss facial expressions in each picture. Point out Rouault's technique of adding layers of color with strong, black lines that give the stained glass effect. Using Rouault's technique, encourage students to express their inner, personal feelings about their artwork.

Project 1

Students will draw their own concept of a clown.

Materials Needed

11" x 14" (28 cm x 36 cm) white drawing paper, pencil, oil pastels

Directions

Use pencil to draw pictures of clowns using thick lines. Color in the areas within the black lines with bright colors. Color heavily, taking care that the colors do not smear. Color the lines with black oil pastel. Go over the lines twice to darken them.

Project 2

Students will draw pictures of themselves or classmates on black paper.

Materials Needed

9" x 12" (23 cm x 30 cm) black construction paper, white glue, assorted pastels, fixative or super-hold hair spray

Directions

Draw portrait on black paper. Outline the pencil drawing with white glue. Let dry. Color using pastels. Spray with fixative or super-hold hair spray.

Render a Clown with Rouault *(cont.)*

Evaluation: Student Interpretation of the Artist's Technique

1. Does the background of the student's picture resemble stained glass?
2. Did the students separate areas with thick lines?
3. Did the students use brilliant colors of crayon and chalk?
4. Did the student portray or reflect pain and misery?
5. Did the student carry the idea throughout the picture?

Test Questions

1. Describe the technique of Georges Rouault.
2. What skill contributed to the development of Rouault's technique?
3. Why is Rouault known as a perfectionist?
4. What were some ideas that Rouault wished to convey with his art?
5. What artistic trend or "ism" best describes Rouault's type of painting?

Answers to Test Questions

1. Georges Rouault used many layers of brightly-colored paint, creating a rich impasto, accented with dark dividing lines to resemble stained glass. He painted with sadness and pity.
2. Rouault was trained, in his youth, to be a maker of stained glass.
3. Rouault worked to make perfect paintings. He destroyed anything he considered unworthy.
4. He wished to express ideas about poverty, war, injustice, and corruption.
5. Rouault is classified as an expressionist.

Sample Project

Originate an Invention with Klee

Life of the Artist

Paul Klee was born near Bern, Switzerland, in 1879. As an adult and an established artist, he moved to Germany where he was commissioned to teach in the Bauhaus School of Design.

Klee had a prolific and intensely curious mind. His experiences and tremendous body of knowledge overflowed into his paintings. He is considered one of the most innovative and greatest pictorial artists of the twentieth century. His mind was even more inventive than the mind of Picasso's. Although his paintings seem very simple, they are actually very complex and not easy to understand.

Klee and two of his well-known artist friends, Wassily Kandinsky and Franz Marc, exhibited their work with the Blue Rider (der Blaue Reiter) group. Even though he was associated with this group, his art remains apart from that or any other established art movement.

When the Nazi's came to power, Klee returned to Switzerland where he spent the remainder of his life creating art. He died in Switzerland in 1940.

Vocabulary

- **whimsical**
  erratic or unpredictable
- **gouache**
  a method of painting with opaque or non-transparent water color; also a pigment
- **fantasy**
  creative imagination; to indulge in reverie
- **Blue Rider (der Blaue Reiter)**
  a group of artists who used shape and color to depict emotion in their paintings
- **childlike**
  marked by simplicity, straight-forwardness, innocence, ingenuousness

Originate an Invention with Klee *(cont.)*

Technique of the Artist

Paul Klee created a phenomenal amount of art in his lifetime. His works number in the thousands. His pictures were usually small and he used a variety of media including pen and ink, watercolor, gouache, and colored pencils. His pictures were a study in the economy of simple lines and the use of delicate color. His drawings were fraught with mystery and contained elements of a make-believe world. Humor and a childlike technique also added to his art. An interesting title completed his work—one necessary to help understand the piece.

Suggestions for a Project

Project 1

Select a print by Paul Klee, such as *The Twittering Machine* or *The Red Balloon* to use as an example of Klee's technique for the students to create their own whimsical pictures.

Materials Needed

9" x 12" (23 cm x 30 cm) white 1" (2.5 cm) graph paper, watercolors, brush, ruler, water cup, newspaper, pencil, paper towels, eraser, markers

Directions

Sketch a whimsical design onto the graph paper. Paint a thin watercolor wash in the background. While the background is slightly damp, add brighter colors so that the edges will be feathery and the brighter colors will blend slightly with the background and give the composition a fuzzy appearance. When dry, outline and color some shapes using colored markers.

Project 2

Study the ancient symbols of the Egyptians or of the Native American. Each student should choose a favorite symbol from books provided by the teacher.

Materials Needed

scrap construction paper; plastic drop cloth; various pastel colors of spray paint; pencil; scissors; 9" x 12" (23 cm x 30 cm) pastel construction paper in various colors

Directions

Choose a favorite symbol to draw, cut out, and use as a stencil. Use scrap construction paper. Lay stencil on the pastel construction paper. Go outdoors and spread a drop cloth. Ask a volunteer helper to spray the page with several colors. Remove and discard symbol to show off the colorful composition.

Originate an Invention with Klee *(cont.)*

Evaluation: Student Interpretation of the Artist's Technique

1. Was the student's drawing innovative?
2. Were there just a few lines simply drawn?
3. Was there a hint of fantasy in the drawing?
4. Was there a touch of humor in the drawing?
5. Was the drawing given a meaningful title?
6. Did the student use delicate color?

Test Questions

1. With what group did Klee exhibit his art?
2. Was Klee's work patterned after any formal art movement? Explain.
3. Why was a title important to Klee's work?
4. Describe some elements of Klee's technique.
5. Why did Klee return to Switzerland?

Answers to Test Questions

1. Klee exhibited with the Blue Rider group.
2. Klee did not pattern his work after any formal art movement. It was different from any other art.
3. A title was important to Klee's work to help the viewer understand it.
4. Klee's work was original and childlike. He used few and simple lines as well as delicate color. His drawings had touches of mystery, fantasy, and humor.
5. Klee moved to Switzerland because of the war. Switzerland was a neutral country, and his homeland.

Sample Project

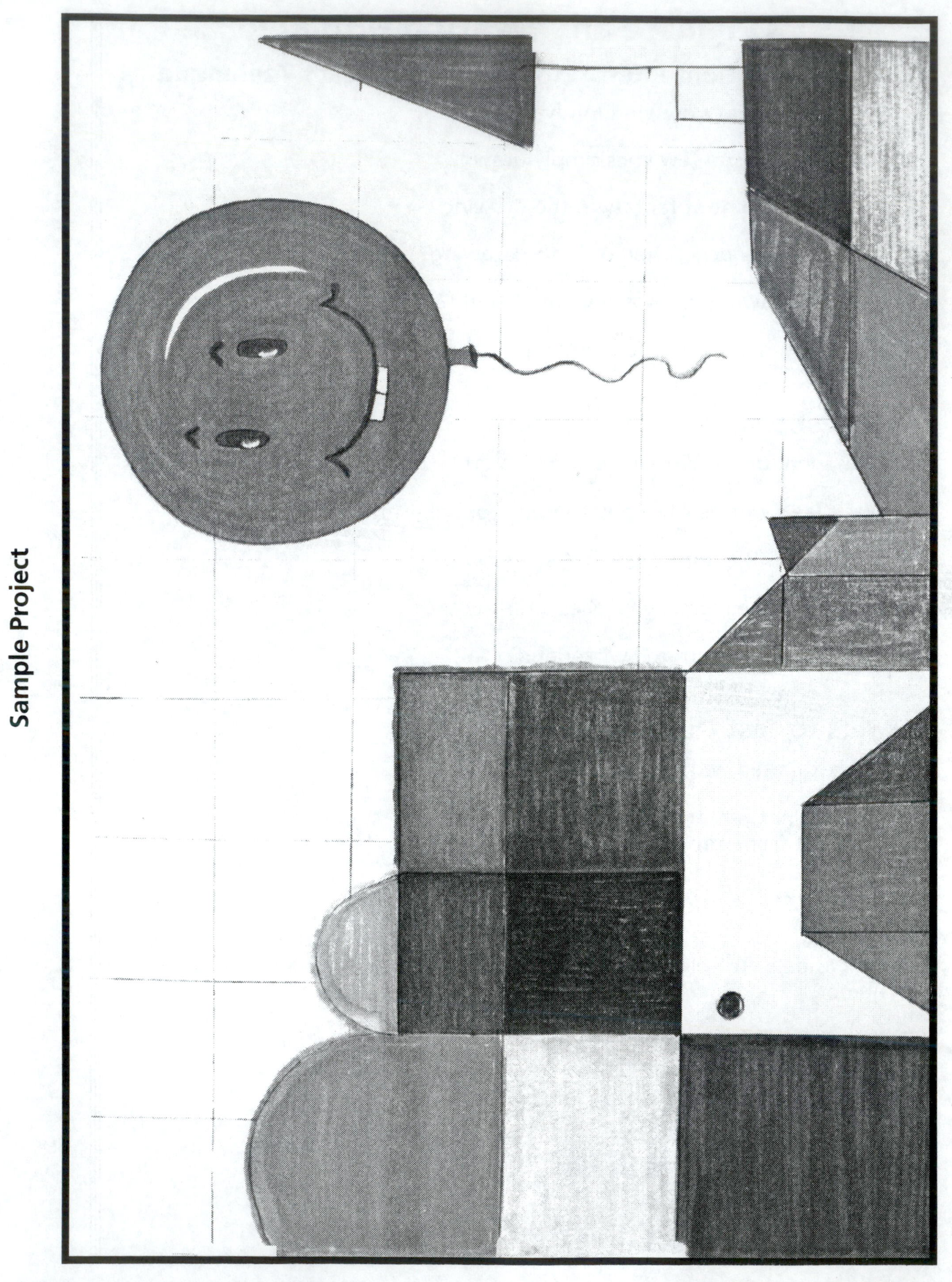

Go Cubic with Pablo Picasso

Life of the Artist

Pablo Picasso was born on October 25, 1881, in Malaga, Spain. He was the son of artist Jose' Ruiz and Maria Picasso Ruiz. Pablo preferred to be known by his mother's maiden name rather than his father's, because Ruiz was a very ordinary surname in that region of Spain.

At the age of five, much to his mother's displeasure, little Pablo scratched drawings of animals on the walls of their home. He drew pictures in wet sand with such skill that his father recognized his talent and arranged for Pablo to take art lessons. Soon his teacher became incensed with Pablo for painting a large sun in the bright red sky.

At the age of fifteen, Pablo was admitted to the Royal Academy in Madrid.

Picasso is probably best known for his work with geometric form. Along with his friend Georges Braque, Picasso invented cubism. The new style distorted and broke up natural objects and people into geometric forms showing a limited resemblance to real objects. Picasso was one of the most influential artists of the twentieth century. His work provided inspiration and a fresh approach to modern artists. He challenged long established ideas, breaking all the rules of traditional art. Picasso died April 8, 1973.

Vocabulary

- **geometric forms**

  Cézanne's advice to Picasso was to "look at nature in terms of spheres, cones and cylinders."

Go Cubic with Pablo Picasso *(cont.)*

Technique of the Artist

Picasso had a variety of techniques, depending on the phases of his art. His early work was traditional, executed in shades of blue and cool colors with a melancholy theme. The paintings were dark and filled with sadness, due to the loss of a friend. This was called his Blue Period.

Later he moved to France. Here, he lightened his palette as he became interested in the clowns and acrobats of the circus. Shades of red crept into his work, as well as happier themes. This was known as his Rose Period.

Later Picasso became interested in African and Iberian art. He dissected the classical idea of art, shattering it into geometric forms like facets on jewels with three-dimensional qualities. Later he added collage until he realized he could get the effect of collage by simply using paint.

Suggestions for a Project

Project

Set up a simple still life using interesting shaped kitchen utensils. Encourage students to draw them with the cubist technique as Picasso did. A second suggestion is to ask students to draw two animals not ordinarily pictured together. (Examples: bear and dolphin, giraffe and whale, bird and manatee, snake and elephant, or other animals of the student's choice.)

Materials Needed

still life with kitchen utensils or books with animal pictures, ruler, 12" x 18" (23 cm x 46 cm) white drawing paper, pencil, eraser, acrylic or tempera paint, brushes, bowl of water, paper towels, firm cardboard, scissors, paste

Directions

Rule a 1" (2.5 cm) frame on the drawing paper. Ask students to sketch lightly the project of their choice. When the sketch is finished, make some of the rounded lines angular. Leave some lines rounded. Students should study Picasso's technique and imitate it. They may add anything they wish. Paint with acrylic or tempera. Mount the painting on firm cardboard.

Go Cubic with Pablo Picasso *(cont.)*

Evaluation: Student Interpretation of the Artist's Technique

1. Did the student use angular lines to give the composition a geometric appearance?
2. Did the student use some curving lines as the cubist's did?
3. Did the students fill the picture plane with the drawing?
4. Does the drawing show careful attention to detail?
5. Is the drawing neatly painted to make a composition that is attractive?

Test Questions

1. What was Picasso's most important contribution to the art world?
2. What artist helped Picasso develop a new style of painting?
3. Explain Picasso's attitude toward the established rules of art.
4. Describe the way Picasso used collage in his paintings.
5. Did Picasso ever use traditional rules of art in his paintings?

Answers to Test Questions

1. Picasso's most important contribution to the art world was the development of cubism.
2. Georges Braque helped Picasso develop cubism.
3. Picasso challenged established rules of art breaking with tradition as he developed innovative ways of expression.
4. Picasso integrated collage into his paintings so that it fit into the theme of the composition.
5. Picasso painted traditionally during the early years of his art education.

Sample Project

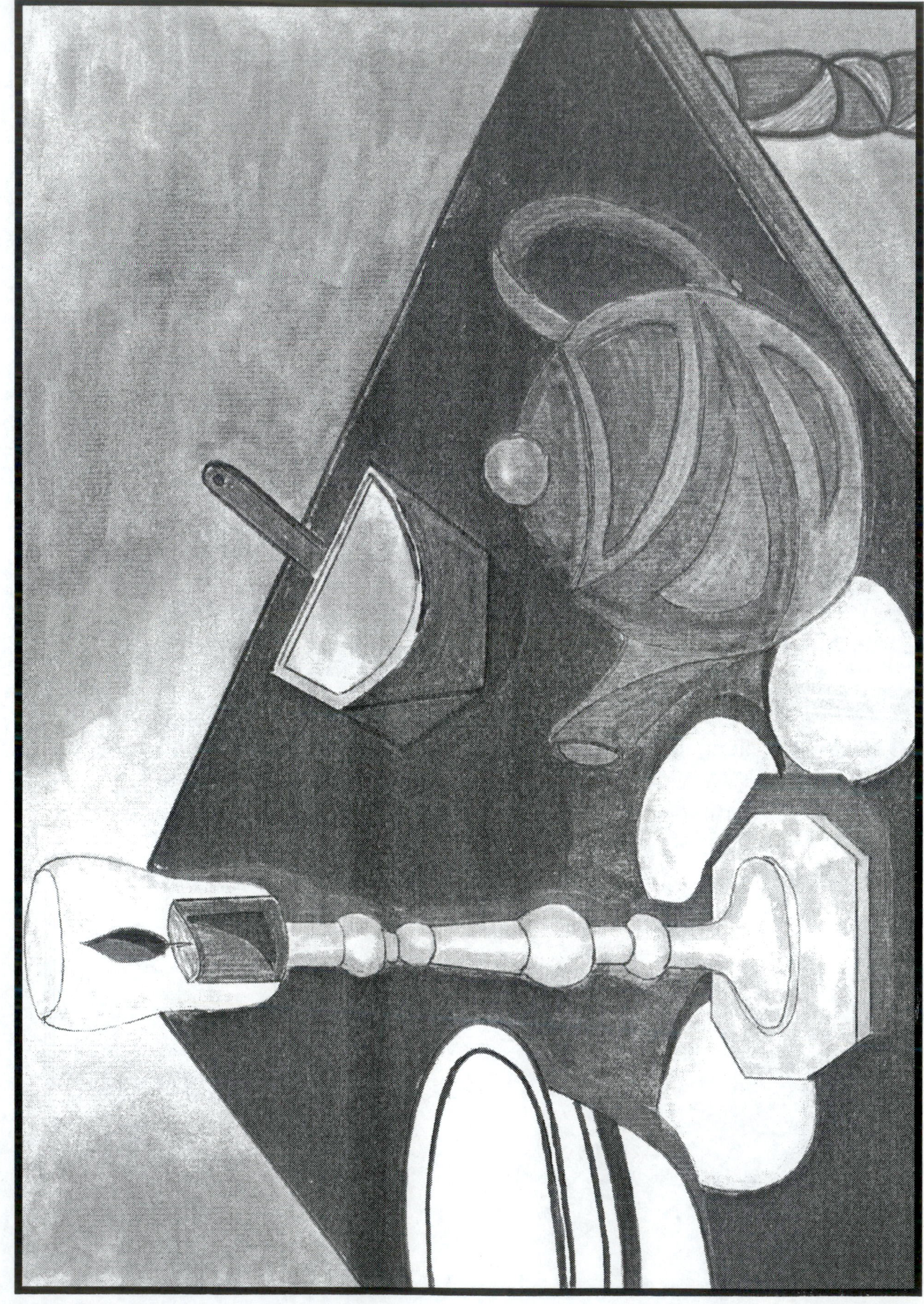

Lock in a Still Life with Braque

Life of the Artist

Georges Braque was born May 13, 1882, in Argenteuil. When he was 11 years old, he attended school in Le Harve. He loved painting and music. Gaston Dufy, the brother of Raoul Dufy, a famous artist, gave him flute lessons. By 1897, he was enrolled in evening classes at the Ecole des Beaux Arts. During the daytime he apprenticed as a house painter and interior decorator.

By 1900, Braque attended drawing classes at the Cours Municipal des Batignolles. In 1902, he was schooled at the Academie Humbert. Always a scholar, he explored the effects of light and perspective and how these elements affected three-dimensional objects captured on a two-dimensional plane.

As he matured as an artist, he and other colleagues were instrumental in developing fauvism. Later, he and Pablo Picasso created a very important art movement known as cubism. At the same time they introduced the use of collage.

As Braque aged, he devoted more time to the creation of still life and much of his time was spent drawing birds and adding texture of many kinds to his pictures. In the last years of his life, he was honored with many important exhibitions. Braque died in Paris in 1963.

Vocabulary

- **coherent light**

  a property of laser light; When it strikes an object, it is reflected in all directions.

- **non-coherent light**

  the light that emanates from an ordinary light bulb

- **three-dimensional**

  an object having height, width, and thickness

- **fourth dimension**

  for Braque, it meant space and its relation to an object

- **fauvisum**

  a group of artists (known as the fauves, or wild beasts) who developed an art movement using brilliant colors and bold distortions

Lock in a Still Life with Braque *(cont.)*

Technique of the Artist

Braque used multiple perspectives and non-coherent lighting to stress the three dimensions of an object, reducing the subject to its simplest form.

The fourth dimension, for Braque, is unlimited space that allows objects to have their unique proportions. These concepts influenced Braque and his friend Picasso to develop cubism, an angular and fragmented technique showing different views of the object simultaneously. In the nature phases of cubism, Braque and Picasso used brighter colors, stenciling, and collage. They connected angular objects into a mass composed of a variety of planes that is remarkably complex. It becomes a view or reality seen concurrently in one dimension.

Suggestions for a Project

Project

Students will choose a favorite musical instrument and some unusual fruits of a variety of shapes to compose a still life. Braque combines realistic drawings with geometric forms.

Materials Needed

12" x 18" (30 cm x 46 cm) white or gray drawing paper, pencil, eraser, ruler, glue, poster board, seed catalogs or old magazines, fabric, scissors, acrylic or tempera paints, brush, water bowl, paper towels

Directions

Imitating Braque's style, students sketch the still life lightly on white or gray paper. Have students plan the areas where they will use collage and label them. Pieces of fruit, clipped from the magazines or catalogs, or draped material may be added. Highlights may also be added with acrylic or tempera paint. When dry, add a poster board frame.

Lock in a Still Life with Braque *(cont.)*

Evaluation: Student Interpretation of the Artist's Technique

1. Did the student show different views of the objects drawn?
2. Did the forms in the drawing have an angular appearance?
3. Did the composition unify the parts into one dimension?
4. Did the student use bright colors?
5. Did the student's use of collage blend with the subject of the composition?

Test Questions

1. Why were light and perspective important elements to Braque and Picasso?
2. What art movement did Braque help develop before he became interested in cubism?
3. Discuss Braque's formal training as an artist.
4. Describe the technique of cubism.
5. Give a definition for the term *collage*.

Answers to Test Questions

1. Braque studied these elements in relation to three-dimensional forms.
2. Braque helped to develop fauvism.
3. Braque attended several well-known French art schools before he became an artist. He also apprenticed as a decorator, which provided him additional experience.
4. Cubism is the technique that allows the viewer to see objects from all sides simultaneously. It is angular and fragmented.
5. A *collage* is an artistic composition which has paper or other material pasted on the surface and integrated into the theme of the picture.

Sample Project

Embrace Elongated Faces with Modigliani

Life of the Artist

Amedeo Modigliani was born in Leghorn, Italy, on July 12, 1884. He was the youngest child of Flaminio and Eugenia Garsin Modigliani. At the time of his birth, the family was very poor. An attack of typhoid in 1898 was the turning point in Modigliani's life, for at that time he was allowed to give up school and become apprentice to a painter in the town of Leghorn.

Somewhere around 1902, one of Modigliani's fellow students introduced him to drugs, which proved to be very detrimental to his health.

He arrived in Paris in 1906, doing some painting, but primarily sculpture, which he continued until 1913 or 1914. After that time, he devoted his time to painting. He exhibited his work in a Salon in 1910, and again in 1917.

Roaming the streets after drinking heavily in inclement weather, he became ill of exposure and died January 24, 1920, at age 36. Modigliani was a true pioneer in exploring and developing a style of painting that was truly unique.

Vocabulary

- **elongated**
  stretched out, lengthened
- **almond-shaped**
  an oval shape with a pointed end
- **pioneer**
  to originate, or take part in the development of something new
- **typhoid (fever)**
  a communicable disease marked by fever, headache, and intestinal inflammation

Embrace Elongated Faces with Modigliani *(cont.)*

Technique of the Artist

Modigliani based most of his drawing on oval or almond shapes. He drew oval heads, long, thin noses, and long swan necks with sloping shoulders. His background areas were softly blended colors.

Suggestions for a Project

Project

Imitating Modigliani's style, students will make a painting of the head of a child or adult, using elongated forms to draw the person.

Materials Needed

9" x 12" (23 cm x 30 cm) white drawing paper, pencil, water, brush, tissues, watercolor paint, pastels, black fine-line pen, tagboard or colored drawing paper, fixative or super-hold hair spray

Directions

Lightly sketch a portrait of an adult or child on white drawing paper. The student may also want to indicate on the background, areas of color to be blended. (When using Modigliani's technique, be sure colors are subdued and well blended with tissue.)

Forms are subtly outlined with a fine-line ink pen. Students may use watercolors or pastels as a medium, or they may choose a combination of both. For example, they may paint the figure and use pastels for the background, or use pastels for the figure and paint the background.

When the art piece is finished and thoroughly dry, spray lightly with a fixative from a distance of at least 12 inches (30 cm). Then mount on tagboard or colored drawing paper. Frames may also be cut from tagboard and covered with an appropriate wall paper pattern or an original pattern the student has designed.

Embrace Elongated Faces with Modigliani *(cont.)*

Evaluation: Student Interpretation of the Artist's Technique

1. Did the student draw an oval head, almond eyes, and other forms?
2. Is the nose long and thin?
3. Does the figure have a long swan neck and sloping shoulders?
4. Did the students subdue and softly blend colors?

Test Questions

1. In what country was Modigliani born?
2. How did Modigliani become interested in art?
3. Describe several elements of Modigliani's technique.
4. What other art form did Modigliani pursue besides painting?
5. Why do we say Modigliani was a true art pioneer?

Answers to Test Questions

1. Modigliani was born in the country of Italy.
2. Modigliani contracted typhoid fever, gave up school at age 14, and was permitted to take art lessons.
3. Modigliani's technique consisted of oval-shaped heads, almond eyes, long, thin noses, long swan necks, and elongated figures.
4. Modigliani was also interested in sculpture. He used the same elongated technique when he worked in stone.
5. Modigliani was a true art pioneer because he invented an entirely new technique.

Sample Project

Rustle up a Mural with Rivera

Life of the Artist

Diego Rivera was born in Guancjuato, Mexico, on December 8, 1886. When he was still a young child, the family moved to Mexico City. He attended the Fine Arts Academy on a government scholarship and was privileged to be taught by a teacher who had been a pupil of Jean-Auguste Dominique Ingres, a well-known artist from the neoclassicist art movement.

He worked for an engraver, José Guadalupe Posada, who influenced him greatly.

Within five years, Diego Rivera had his first exhibition, which was a great success. This earned him a scholarship in Spain. Later he moved to Paris and was influenced by Paul Cézanne. He investigated cubism and other art movements.

Rivera returned to Mexico in 1921 and became influential in reviving the art of mural painting. Through his art, Rivera made statements about the social problems as well as the history of Mexico. He painted murals on the walls of many public buildings. He also painted frescoes in the Auditorium of the National Agricultural School at Chapingo, which is an example of some of his finest work. He is known as one of the most talented artists Mexico has ever given to the world. Besides his art, Diego Rivera was active in Mexican politics. He died in his studio in Mexico City on November 24, 1957.

Vocabulary

- **mural**
  a wall painting or panorama
- **post modernism**
  the last four decades of the twentieth century
- **Pre-Cortesian**
  before the conquest of Mexico by Cortes in 1519

Rustle up a Mural with Rivera *(cont.)*

Technique of the Artist

Diego Rivera was a superior draftsman with an acute sense of dynamic composition. He painted murals in bright colors, but in pleasing tones, and always harmoniously placed. He liked historical and rural themes, which he integrated with social commentary.

Post-modernism and cubism were used by Diego Rivera. He revived fresco, but avoided the European style of painting. He was fascinated by Pre-Cortesian art and native imagery as well as the love of nature.

Suggestions for a Project

Project

Students draw a mural of a farm scene with barnyard, fields, tractor, etc., or a park scene with people picnicking, golfing, children having fun on playground equipment, etc., or another panoramic scene of their choice.

Materials Needed

two pieces of 9" x 12" (23 cm x 30 cm) white drawing paper per student, tempera or acrylic paint, brushes, bowl of water, paper towels, eraser, pencil, paste, ruler, tagboard or Bristol board

Directions

On one piece of drawing paper, draw a line on the 9" (23 cm) edge the width of the ruler (about 1" [2.5 cm] wide). Apply paste and lay the other piece of drawing paper on its edge touching the line drawn. Let dry. Each student now has a 9" x 25" (23 cm x 63 cm) working surface.

Students pencil in a panoramic scene of a suggested subject or may choose any subject appropriate to the mural. Have them paint with bright, slightly shaded colors as Diego Rivera did. When thoroughly dry, mount on tagboard or Bristol board. Clip off edges of mounting board even with the edge of the picture.

Rustle up a Mural with Rivera *(cont.)*

Evaluation: Student Interpretation of the Artist's Technique

1. Did the student draw a true panoramic scene?
2. Did the student draw several interesting groupings of activities in the scene?
3. Did the student use bright but slightly shaded colors?
4. Is it easy to see the overall theme of the mural?
5. Did the student imitate Diego Rivera's style?

Test Questions

1. Give a definition for the word *mural*.
2. What is meant by "social commentary"?
3. What were two favorite themes Diego Rivera chose to paint?
4. Name two places you might find Diego Rivera's murals.
5. Name two art movements that were favorites of Diego Rivera.

Answers to Test Questions

1. A *mural* is a panoramic scene often painted on the outside of a building.
2. Rivera's paintings often criticized problems in society.
3. Rivera's two favorite themes were historical and rural scenes.
4. Rivera's murals were often on the outside walls of buildings or sometimes inside public buildings.
5. Two art styles that interested Rivera were the post-modernism and cubist styles.

Sample Project

Mastering Movement with Marcel

Life of the Artist

Marcel Duchamp was born on July 28, 1887, near Rouen, France. The family had a strong interest in the arts. His brother was a well known sculptor and his sister was equally well-known as a poetess. He began to paint as early as 1908 and during his lifetime, he influenced many art movements, including fada, fauvism, and cubism. He was internationally a singular factor in the development of avant-garde art.

Duchamp's most famous work is *Nude Descending the Staircase No. 2*. It gives the viewer the feeling of continuous movement by presenting a series of similar cubistic overlapping figures. It is reminescent of a series of photos of a moving object.

Marcel Duchamp blazed new trails in art when he invented kinetic art, and again with his concept of "readymades." His "readymades" were everyday objects to which he assigned a new function. Kinetic art was either drawn to show movement or actual three-dimensional forms which were capable of movement. An example is a bicycle wheel mounted on a stool.

Marcel Duchamp had a profound influence on the artists of America with his charming personality and innovative ways. In 1955, he became an American citizen. He died on October 1, 1968.

Vocabulary

- **avant-garde**

  a French word relating to new or experimental methods in the arts

- **kinetic art**

  art that is in motion, such as a mobile; art that implies motion on a two-dimensional plane

- **intellectual response**

  Duchamp believed that art should not be created from observation. Rather, it should be conceived and created by the mind.

- **dada**

  an artistic movement based on deliberate irrationality and negation of the laws of beauty and organization

Mastering Movement with Marcel *(cont.)*

Technique of the Artist

Duchamp used complex planes and geometric shapes along with muted colors in his paintings.

He focused on the visual effects of art. The manipulation of shapes interested him. He was dedicated to the avant-garde and experimentation. Duchamp decried observation and favored intellectual response in all of his innovations.

Suggestions for a Project

Project

Complete a composition showing movement as Marcel Duchamp did. It could be a scene from everyday life such as taking the student's pet for a walk, a sports event, a bicycle ride, or other subjects of the student's choice.

Materials Needed

five muted colors of construction paper (e.g., red, yellow, blue, orange, and green); 12" x 18" (23 cm x 46 cm) white construction paper (two sheets per student); assorted colored markers or paint; scissors; pencil; eraser; thin, black magic marker; black ballpoint pen

Directions

On white 12" x 18" (23 cm x 46 cm) paper, draw a simple action figure of the student's choice. Cut it out and use the action figure as a pattern to cut five figures from five muted colors of construction paper. Mount the figures diagonally on a piece of 12" x 18" (23 cm x 46 cm) paper, overlapping the figures to show action, as Marcel Duchamp did.

Paste the figures down securely. Sketch background scenery and color it with markers, or paint the scene if you wish. Add features on the cutouts with thin, black marker and ballpoint pen.

Mastering Movement with Marcel *(cont.)*

Evaluation: Interpretation of the Artist's Technique

1. Did the student show movement in the compositions?
2. Did the student add geometric forms?
3. Did the student use muted colors?
4. As a whole, is the composition attractive?
5. Does the composition show originality and innovation?

Test Questions

1. How did Marcel Duchamp influence American artists?
2. What was Marcel Duchamp's most famous painting?
3. What art movement is evidenced in Marcel Duchamp's famous painting?
4. What was "readymade art"?
5. What was Marcel Duchamp's idea about how one should create an art piece?

Answers to Test Questions

1. Marcel Duchamp influenced American artists with his innovative art creations, as well as his charming personality.
2. Marcel Duchamp's most famous painting was *Nude Descending a Staircase, No. 2*.
3. Marcel Duchamp's famous painting is an example of Cubism.
4. Marcel Duchamp invented "readymade" art by taking ordinary objects and assigning a new function to them.
5. Marcel Duchamp thought that designing art pieces should come from the mind, rather than from observation with the eyes.

Sample Project

Be Enthralled with Chagall

Life of the Artist

Marc Chagall was born on July 7, 1887, in Vitseybsk, Russia. He came from a devout Jewish family and attended Jewish elementary school. He became interested in art at school and furthered his study with a private teacher. He later studied at St. Petersburg, and it was during this time that he painted rather bizarre, nightmarish pictures.

In 1915, he married Bella Rosenfeld. She appears in many of his paintings.

In 1920, Chagall went to Paris, where he moved into a Bohemian artist colony. Here he met artists on their way to becoming famous. Among them were Leger, Delaunay, and Soutine. Chagall was inspired by these artists and did some of his best work during his years in France.

Chagall was a pioneer in developing psychic reality. He used fantasy, reality, and nostalgia in his compositions. He often placed his figures upside down, sometimes superimposed on another figure, or overlapping, further suggesting psychic reality. Under the influence of the art movements of this time, he began using brighter colors, not garish, but toned into a harmonious and complementary composition. In many paintings, Chagall recalls memories from his childhood in a Russian village. Chagall died on March 28, 1985, in France.

Vocabulary

- **Bohemian artist colony**
  a group of artists living an unconventional life
- **psychic reality**
  a reality outside the sphere of physical science
- **pioneeer**
  to originate or take part in the development of something new; to go first

Be Enthralled with Chagall *(cont.)*

Technique of the Artist

Chagall's technique is a combination of French cubism and Russian expressionism. Marc Chagall reminisces in his paintings of Russian village scenes, biblical scenes, themes from literary classics, and of his personal life. His style is childlike; his subject matter is rendered with dreamlike simplicity in strong, bright colors. Explaining his technique, Chagall said, "I work with whatever medium likes me at the moment."

Suggestions for a Project

Project

Students will use memories from the past to make a composition of a dream or a nightmare.

Materials Needed

9" x 12" (23 cm x 30 cm) white or pale mauve construction paper, pencil, eraser, bowl of water, paper towels, brush, compass, ruler, tempera or acrylic paint, paste, scissors, cardboard or tagboard for frame

Directions

On the construction paper draw a dream or nightmare as Chagall did. Notice that Chagall mixes organic forms with geometric forms. His colors are bright but not gaudy; his forms mix reality with fantasy. Students should use their imagination to compose a dreamlike composition. Mount on cardboard, tagboard, or in a shadow box.

Be Enthralled with Chagall *(cont.)*

Evaluation: Student Interpretation of the Artist's Technique

1. Did the student's composition give the viewer the feeling of a dream or nightmare?
2. Did the student use bright colors?
3. Were some of the figures upside down?
4. Does the composition seem to tell a fragmented story?
5. Are some figures superimposed on other figures?
6. Is the composition attractive? Are the colors and forms well placed?

Test Questions

1. Name three things in Chagall's pictures that would help identify his technique in other paintings by the artist.
2. In what city did Chagall do his best work?
3. Who was it that appearered in many of his paintings?
4. Why is Chagall called a pioneer?
5. In what country did Chagall live most of his life?

Answers to Test Questions

1. Any three of the following answers would be acceptable: bright colors, upside-down figures, small genre scenes, biblical scenes, dreamlike quality, village scenes, fantasy quality.
2. Chagall did his best work in Paris.
3. It was Bella Rosenfeld, his wife.
4. Chagall is called a pioneer because he was one of the first to put psychic reality into his pictures.
5. Chagall lived most of his life in France.

Sample Project

Cook up a Compostion with Chang Dai-chien

Life of the Artist

Chang was born in Nei-chiang, Szechwan, as Chuan Chi on May 19, 1899. When he was 19 years old, he began studying painting and calligraphy with well-known Chinese artists in Shanghai. In 1925, Chang's family suffered severe financial losses. Several family businesses were lost, depriving Chang of his income. It is for this reason that Chang decided to sell his artwork.

His first exhibition, in 1926, was a great success, and as a result, he became well known.

In 1937, the Sino-Japanese War forced him to find a new location to pursue his career. He settled in a desert refuge of Ten Huang where he studied and copied murals in the Caves of the Thousand Buddahs.

The Civil War of 1949 forced Chang to move again. This time he settled outside of Sao, Brazil, where a flood destroyed his home. In 1967, he moved to the Monterey Peninsula. During the late '60s and most of the '70s, Chang invented the technique known as "splash color and splash ink." In 1967, he moved to Taiwan.

Often called the "Picasso of China," Chang has the reputation for being the best known Chinese painter of the twentieth century. Not only is he famous for his original works, but he is also infamous for illegally copying works of other Chinese artists. Chang Dai-chien died in 1983.

Vocabulary

- **abstract expressionism**

  It is a style of painting developed in Europe and America after World War II. A more understandable concept is "action painting," which encompasses great freedom in electing materials and subject choices, as well as spontaneity in technique and recording the artist's deepest feelings for the composition as a whole.

Cook up a Compostion with Chang Dai-chien

(cont.)

Technique of the Artist

Chang fused together in his paintings, cultures from the Far East and from the West. He also blended parts of Chinese art history with contemporary elements. Forms are well defined; the painting is flat. Chang's colors are vibrant. Some colors have a transparent quality. His technique is reminiscent of abstract expressionism.

Suggestions for a Project

Project

Students will choose a favorite tree and one or more favorite flowers. Then they will combine these forms into a pleasing composition, in the style of Chang.

Materials Needed

books with a variety of trees and flowers, 9" x 12" (23 cm x 30 cm) white or pastel drawing paper, pencil, eraser, scissors, bowl of water, paper towels, water colors, brush, rulers, glue, dark construction paper for mounting, 9" x 12" (23 x 30 cm) or larger

Directions

On the drawing paper, students pencil in a composition with one tree and one or more varieties of flowers. When the composition is complete, students choose three colors of paint to complete the composition. They may use as many shades and tints of these three colors, as desired. (To make shades, add black; to make tints, add white.) When ready to apply the paint, have students dampen the entire sheet of the composition. A wet paper towel will dampen it evenly. Paper that is too damp may be pressed between sheets of dry paper toweling. The students apply watercolor, allowing the color to spread and bleed slightly out of the lines of the drawing. Paint can be controlled with a damp brush. The finished drawing is mounted on dark paper. This process is known as the "wet into wet" technique.

Cook up a Compostion with Chang Dai-chien *(cont.)*

Evaluation: Student Interpretation of the Artist's Technique

1. Are the student's forms clearly defined?
2. Does the painting seem to have a flat quality?
3. Do some areas seem to be transparent?
4. Does the painting have an Oriental quality?
5. Did the student limit his/her colors to three?

Test Questions

1. What event in Chang's life helped him to become well known?
2. Th whom is Chang often compared in America?
3. What technique did Chang invent?
4. What did Chang do to become infamous?
5. Comment on Chang's use of color.

Answers to Test Questions

1. When Chang's family suffered severe financial losses, Chang sold his paintings and became a great success in the art world.
2. Chang is often compared to Picasso, and is known as the "Picasso of China."
3. Chang invented "splash color and splash ink."
4. Chang became infamous when he began to copy Chinese masterpieces.
5. Chang paints with flat color, and his colors are usually vibrant. Some areas have a transparent quality. His use of color shows the freedom of abstract expressionism.

Sample Project

Assemble an Abstract with Lee Krasner

Life of the Artist

Lee Krasner was born in Brooklyn, New York, in 1908 to Russian-Jewish immigrants who provided her with a rich cultural background. At a very young age, Lee wanted to be an artist. She worked as a waitress and as an artist's model to pay for her education at Cooper Union and the National Academy of Design.

She gained inspiration by viewing works by Picasso and Matisse, which were on exhibit at the Museum of Modern Art.

During the Great Depression, she painted murals for the WPA. Krasner met the Dutch artist, Piet Mondrian, who encouraged her to explore the new technique of abstract expressionism. During this time, she joined American Abstract Artists, which promoted non-representational art. She also studied with Hans Hoffman to further develop her abstract studies.

In 1942, she met the artist Jackson Pollock while some of her works were on exhibit. The artists married in 1945, setting up residence in East Hampton where each had a studio. For many years, Lee promoted her husband's work while she remained in the shadow of his genius. She had a hard time establishing herself as an artist due to discrimination in the 1940s. At that time, women were expected to stay at home, raise a family, and leave careers to the men. Through the years, Krasner has come to be appreciated and honored for the excellence of her own work.

Vocabulary

- **AAA (American Abstract Artists)**
  a group that promotes abstract art
- **WPA (Works Progress Administration)**
  an emergency program set up by President Roosevelt to give aid to the victims of the Great Depression; It provided work for eight million people.
- **abstract expressionism (Krasner's version)**
  paint "subconsciously" without drawing, with great freedom of the use of heavy lines, spots, drips, and smudges

Assemble an Abstract with Lee Krasner *(cont.)*

Technique of the Artist

As a young adult, Krasner's work was realistic, but she soon used surrealist forms and blended them into a cubistic technique. Later she took linear forms and added them to colorful backgrounds. She liked to use a repetition of lines and shapes, as well as the contrast of light and dark areas, creating a definite rhythm of forms in the style of abstract expressionism. She also liked to do "little image painting," in which she used small calligraphic shapes that were repeated rhythmically and depicted high energy.

Suggestions for a Project

Project

After studying Krasner's paintings, students will use a calligraphy book and choose some ornate alphabet letters as a basis for an abstract expressionist composition. (*Note to teacher:* A copy of ornate alphabet letters for each student will help them use their imagination and creative abilities to the fullest.)

Materials Needed

four 8" (20-cm) square light weight cardboard or poster boards; multi-colored acrylic paint in bottles with small dispenser caps; water cup; brushes; paper towels; newspaper; paint palette; pencil; calligraphy book and copy sheets for students; metal hangers or paper clips for hanging; colored cardboard or tagboard

Directions

Students pencil in an idea lightly on the four poster boards (each with a different design) and then squeeze paint from the bottles to make shapes on the boards. Lines and shapes should be thick. Let dry overnight. Paint in the shapes using thinned acrylic paint. Make some areas brighter than others. Leave some background showing. When composition is dry, students may add other lines in a contrasting color, if desired. Mount on heavy colored cardboard or tagboard, leaving a thin border around each piece. Attach hangers and hang as a wall grouping.

Assemble an Abstract with Lee Krasner *(cont.)*

Evaluation: Student Interpretation of the Artist's Technique

1. Did the student use repetition of shapes?
2. Did the student make rhythm and high energy in his/her shapes and lines?
3. Did the student create light and dark areas?
4. Did the student allow some of the background to show?
5. Did the student make thick lines and outline shapes with thick lines?

Test Questions

1. What work did Lee Krasner do to earn money for her education as an artist?
2. How does the term *abstract expressionism* relate to the art style of Lee Krasner?
3. Which two artists helped and encouraged Krasner to explore abstract expressionism?
4. Why did Lee Krasner promote the art of her husband, Jackson Pollock, rather than her own?
5. For what did the organization AAA stand, and what did it promote?

Answers to Test Questions

1. Lee Krasner worked as a waitress and an artist's model to further her education.
2. Lee Krasner chose the freedom of abstract expressionism because she wanted to create art spontaneously, with unplanned areas in her compositions. *Note to the teacher*: The students (unlike Krasner) have been asked to pencil in lines for their drawings because it takes great skill to create her technique.
3. The Dutch artist, Piet Mondrian encouraged her; she also studied with Hans Hoffman.
4. Women in the 1940s were discriminated against. It was difficult to promote herself.
5. The American Abstract Artist's group promoted abstract art.

Sample Project

Create a Collage with Bearden

Life of the Artist

Romare Bearden was born in Charlotte, North Carolina, on September 2, 1912. After a short time, the family moved to New York City's Harlem.

While still a young man, Romare studied art with the eminent painter, George Grosz. He helped other African-American artists living in Harlem with his knowledge and expertise. Bearden's work was interrupted during World War II while he served in the army. After the war, he studied in Paris at the Sorbonne. His work was influenced by artists he met, including Baldwin, Brancusi, and Brague.

In the 1960s, Bearden was profoundly influenced by the Civil Rights Movement. His art reflects this influence. Romare is best known for his wonderful collage creations, in remembrance of his childhood heritage in the South. His works deal primarily with the African-American experience.

He has always generously helped African-American students further their careers in the art field. He directed the Harlem Cultural Council, organized an art gallery, and was the co-author of a book, *The Painter's Mind*. In 1987, he received the National Medal of Arts from President Reagan.

He died in New York on March 12, 1988.

Vocabulary

- **collage**
  an artistic composition incorporating cut or torn paper fragments pasted on the surface of a picture
- **semi-abstract**
  a composition in which the subject matter is stylized and simplified, but is still recognizable
- **polymer**
  a chemical reaction in which two or more small molecules combine to form larger molecules, as in paints or glazes

Create a Collage with Bearden *(cont.)*

Technique of the Artist

Romare Bearden liked to combine cut or torn paper shapes with polymer paint, adding landscape elements to complete a composition. He used photostats and photocopies along with African masks and people's faces, and hands. He sometimes combined these with vibrant tropical color.

He then applied thin washes to oil paint to mute the tones of the collage shapes. Bearden's semi-abstract collage style has caused him to be regarded as one of the preeminent creators of collage in the United States. His love of learning has helped him incorporate dynamic themes and techniques from other countries.

Suggestions for a Project

Project

Choose a subject that appeals to students, or allow them to choose their own. Some suggestions include a scene from history, Columbus sailing to the New World, and a king on his throne; a queen with her ladies in waiting; an 1890s picnic or modern scene from everyday life. Design a composition using collage and paint in the style of Romare Bearden.

Materials Needed

white or colored drawing paper, pencil, eraser, paint, paintbrush, water, water container, scissors, old magazines, egg carton, white glue, clear plastic finishing spray (optional)

Directions

Sketch a scene of choice on drawing paper. Lightly pencil in areas of color. Find collage pictures that relate to the theme of the drawing. Cut out and position them loosely on your composition, until a pleasing effect is achieved. Paste down the pictures securely with white glue. Add paint in designated areas. A thin wash of color will lend continuity to the composition. When the scene is completely dry (overnight is best), it may be lightly sprayed with clear plastic spray. Add a frame or mount the picture on colored paper.

Create a Collage with Bearden *(cont.)*

Evaluation: Interpretation of the Artist's Technique

1. Did the student complete a meaningful and attractive scene?
2. Did the student use a combination of paint and magazine clippings effectively?
3. Were the pictures chosen by the students appropriate to the chosen scene?
4. Was the composition colorful?
5. Did the student fill the page without leaving too much negative space?

Test Questions

1. For what kind of art is Bearden best known?
2. Explain the meaning of *semi-abstract art*.
3. What impressed you most about Bearden's life?
4. How did President Reagan honor Bearden?
5. Explain the technique of Romare Bearden.

Answers to Test Questions

1. Bearden is best known for combining collage and paint in his compositions.
2. *Semi-abstract art* is simplified and stylized so that the forms are abstract but are still recognized.
3. Answers are subjective.
4. President Reagan honored Romare Bearden by bestowing on him the National Medal of the Arts.
5. Romare Bearden's subject matter was, for the most part, African-American. He combined collage and paint in a truly creative way, using vivid colors and then washing to blend the elements of the picture.

Sample Project

Sketch a Sporting Event with de Kooning

Life of the Artist

Elaine Fried was born in New York in 1920. At an early age she was influenced by her mother's love of art. From the time of elementary school, she planned to be an artist. With her mother's encouragement, she studied at two important art schools. Later, she took private art lessons from well-known artist Willem de Kooning. Five years later, Elaine and Willem were married.

Elaine's interests were very broad, especially in the art world. She enjoyed drawing and painting sports figures, which she gleaned from newspaper accounts. Bull fighting fascinated her and she liked to paint portraits. She was commissioned by President Kennedy to paint his portrait, but he was killed before the time could be arranged.

Elaine also wrote articles for *ARTnews* magazine and taught fine art classes at the University of New Mexico. She died on February 1, 1989.

Vocabulary

- **stylized**
  to design according to a style rather than according to nature
- **negative space**
  empty space used to enhance art forms
- **finger paint**
  usually a water-based paint of a creamy consistency that is applied with the fingers

Sketch a Sporting Event with de Kooning *(cont.)*

Technique of the Artist

Elaine tended to use intense colors with vigorous brushwork, along with ample negative space; her compositions had a finger-paint quality. Her vigorous and seemingly careless use of oil color to create a highly stylized interpretation of an event is actually very carefully planned and well executed.

Suggestions for a Project

Project

Using Elaine Fried de Kooning's technique, students will draw a sporting event or a portrait of themselves or a classmate.

Materials Needed

six or more small glass jars or a plastic egg carton for paint; washable finger paint in several colors; white finger-paint paper; large construction paper for frame; pencil; eraser; paper towels; bowl of water; brushes; cotton swabs and other household items to create texture; scissors; ruler

Directions

Students sketch lightly on finger-paint paper a sporting event or a portrait. Then they apply finger paint carefully and spread with fingers. They may use swabs, brushes, etc. to achieve pleasing textures where needed. When finished, let paintings dry overnight. Students then mount their finished art on contrasting construction paper or cut a suitable frame for the composition.

Sketch a Sporting Event with de Kooning *(cont.)*

Evaluation: Student Interpretation of the Artist's Technique

1. Did the student use finger paint creatively?
2. Is there an identifiable pictorial element in the picture?
3. Did the student use a variety of interesting textures in the picture?
4. Is the picture at least somewhat abstract?
5. Is the picture well mounted or framed in an appropriate color to enhance the picture?

Test Questions

1. Who was responsible for Elaine Fried de Kooning's interest in art?
2. Name two kinds of pictures Elaine liked to paint.
3. Describe Elaine Fried de Kooning's painting technique.
4. To whom was Elaine married?
5. Besides painting, what were two other kinds of work Elaine did?

Answers to Test Questions

1. Elaine Fried de Kooning's mother was responsible for her interest in art.
2. Elaine liked to paint portraits and sports figures.
3. Elaine's painting technique was seemingly careless, but it was really well planned.
4. Elaine was married to artist Willem de Kooning.
5. Elaine taught art on the college level and wrote articles on art for *ARTnews* magazine.

Sample Project

Concoct Quality Textures with Quang Ho

Life of the Artist

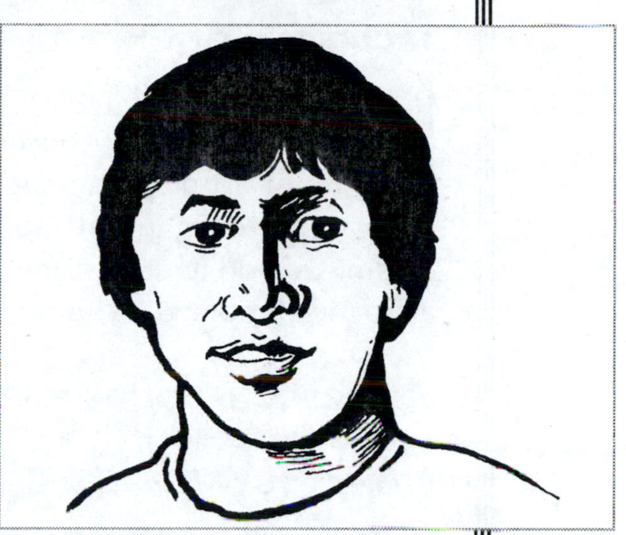

Quang Ho was born in Hue, Vietnam, in 1963. When he was four years old, signs of his artistic talent were evident. During the Tet Offensive in 1968, his father was imprisoned by the North Vietnamese. In April 1975, Quang's mother and her eight children left for America, just before Saigon fell to the enemy.

When Quang was 19 years old, his mother was killed in an automobile accident. Quang and his older sister took responsibility for the family.

Quang graduated from high school and attended The Colorado Institute of Art on a scholarship. He became a successful freelance illustrator until he began to concentrate solely on fine art.

"I like to allow each painting to tell me . . . how it needs to be painted individually and not to rely on any particular technique or method of painting I'm comfortable with."

Today Quang works in galleries across the United States. He teaches art class in Denver once a week. Collectors who wish to buy a painting have been on a waiting list for three years. A waiting list of two years is necessary to enter one of his art classes.

Vocabulary

- **illustrator**
  a person who makes something clear by means of a picture or diagram
- **composition**
  the act of arranging forms into an artistic creation
- **carefree brushwork**
  the act of applying brushwork so that it seems unplanned
- **texture**
  as it is used here, it is the roughness or smoothness of the surface of a painting

Concoct Quality Textures with Quang Ho *(cont.)*

Technique of the Artist

Quang Ho exhibited a great feeling for individuality in every picture. His artwork shows careful concentration on composition and the correct blending of art elements such as shape, texture, value, color, line, etc. Quang Ho was masterful in putting together several diverse textures such as glass, ceramic, wood, water, stone, and live plants and organizing them into an attractive whole with light and shadow.

Suggestions for a Project

Project

Students will compose a still life with many textures.

Example: Draw a ceramic teapot filled with yellow dandelions and purple thistles sitting on a roughly woven tablecloth. Place several pieces of fruit in the picture, such as a shiny red apple, dimple-skinned limes, a lemon, and an interesting glass bottle. There are many other new and refreshing ideas students may have in their imaginations.

Materials Needed

acrylic paints, water, brush, paper towels, water container, 9" x 12" (23 cm x 30 cm) white and colored construction paper, paste, pencil, scissors, textured wallpaper, glossy plastic spray, book with pictures of plants and weeds, ruler, fabric

Directions

Cut the white paper to a size of 7" x 10" (18 cm x 25 cm). Students will compose a still life with many different textures in it, using the entire picture plane for the composition. Have them take their time and work carefully to make the composition truly unique.

From textured wallpaper, a variety of fruit and other shapes may be cut and pasted onto the composition. Using acrylic paint, students color the fruit, allowing the texture of the wallpaper to simulate fruit skin. Fabric may be used for a drape or tablecloth, if desired.

When the composition is finished, spray with glossy plastic spray, or block out the background and spray the fruit with the glossy spray, leaving the background and some of the forms with a matte finish. When dry, mount on colored construction paper with a 1" (2.5 cm) margin around the composition.

Concoct Quality Textures with Quang Ho *(cont.)*

Evaluation: Student Interpretation of the Artist's Technique

1. Did the student have a well thought-out composition?
2. Did the student achieve satisfactory spatial tension between elements of the picture?
3. Did the student's brushwork add texture?
4. Was the brushwork carefree?
5. Did the overall composition show care and originality?
6. Were the various textures organized into a dynamic composition?
7. Were the colors distributed attractively?

Test Questions

1. Where was Quang Ho born?
2. What did Quang Ho want his paintings to tell him?
3. List some textures Ho used.
4. Why do you think Ho's paintings are popular?
5. Why does Ho use different techniques when he paints?

Answers to Test Questions

1. Quang Ho was born in Hue, Vietnam.
2. Quang wanted his paintings to tell him how they should be painted.
3. Quang Ho used glass, ceramic, stone, wood, water, plant life, etc.
4. His paintings are popular because of his attention to making an interesting composition, the choice of unusual objects as subject matter, and the careful selection of colors and textures. Answers will vary.
5. Quang Ho uses different techniques in painting because different subject matter seems to lend itself to different techniques.

Sample Project

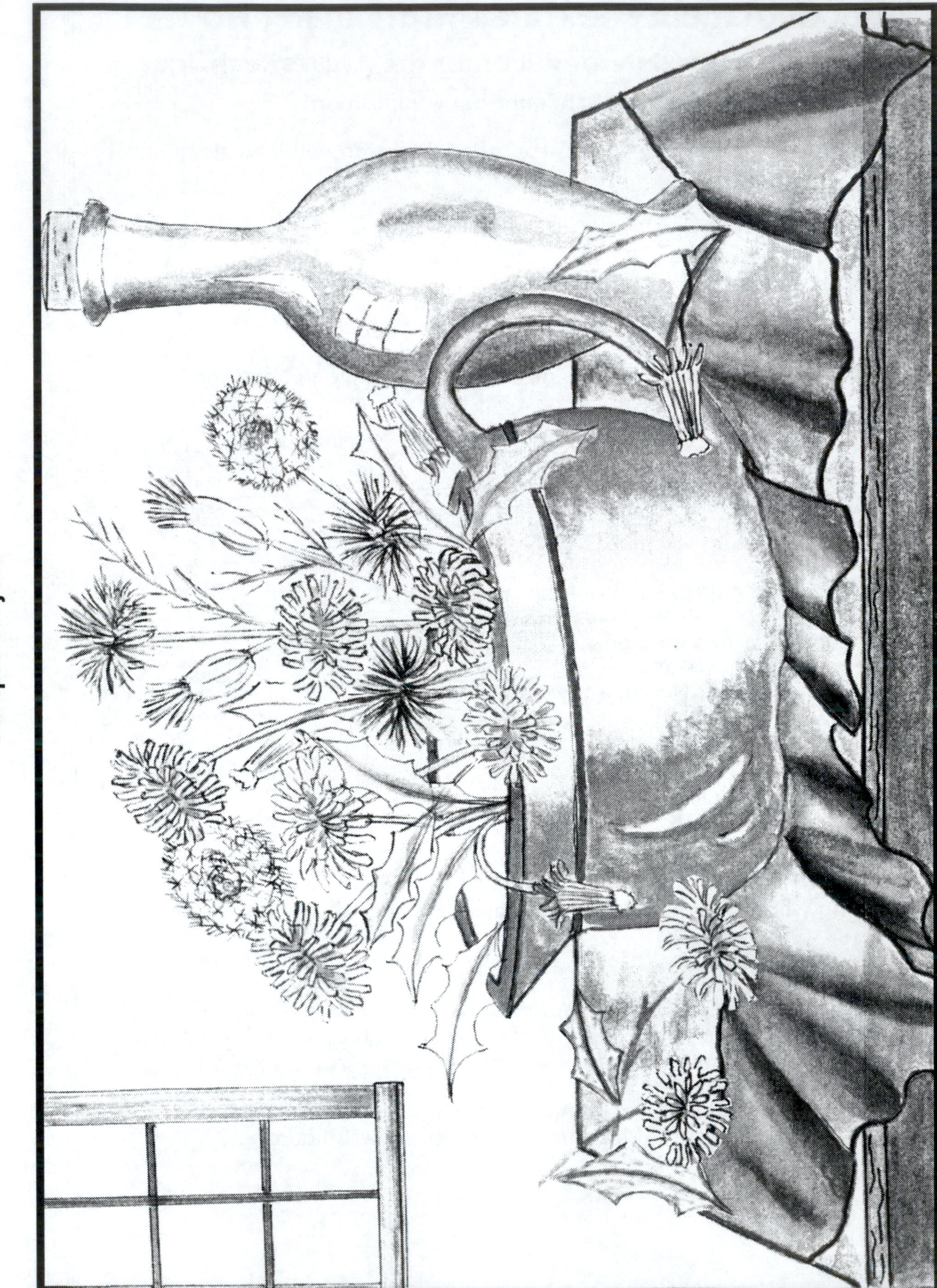

Artist ______________________________ Date ______________

Title: ____

Life of the Artist

Vocabulary

Technique of the Artist

Suggestions for a Project

Project

Materials Needed

Directions

Evaluation: Interpretation of the Artist's Technique

1.

2.

3.

4.

5.

Test Questions

1.

2.

3.

4.

5.

Answers to Test Questions

1.

2.

3.

4.

5.

Bibliography

Books

Bahn, Paul G. and Jean Vertut. *Images of the Ice Age.* New York: Facts on File, 1998.

Bandi, Hans-George et al. *The Art of the Stone Age.* New York: Crown Publishers, Inc., 1990.

Bertelli, Carlo, Editor. *Mosaics*. New York: Gallery Books, 1988.

Cogniat, Raymond. *Braque*. New York: Harry N. Abrams, Inc., 1980.

Diamondstein, Barbarlee, Ed. *The Art World.* New York: Art News Books, 1977.

Flening, William. *Arts and Ideas.* New York: Holt, Rinehart and Winston, 1986.

Gombrich, Ernest. *The Story of Art.* London: Phaidon Press, Ltd., 1995.

Hall, Douglas. *Modigliana*. London: Phaidon Press, Ltd., 1979.

Heller, Nancy G. *Women Artists: An Illustrated History.* New York: Abbeville Press, 1987.

Kellir, Jane. *Grandma Moses: 25 Masterworks.* New York: Harry N. Abrams, Inc., 1997.

Janson, H. W. with Dora Jane Janson. *History of Art.* New Jersey: Prentice Hall and New York: Harry N. Abrams, Inc. 1965.

Stechow, Wolfgang. *Bruegel*. New York: Harry N. Abrams, Inc., 1940 and 1968.

References

Microsoft Encarta '97

The World Book Encyclopedia. Chicago: Filed Enterprises Educational Corporation, 1970.

Web Sites

More information on the artists and their artwork can be found by doing a search on various Internet search engines.

